The Power of One

The Power of One

Leading with Civility, Candor, and Courage

Natasha Bowman, J.D.

Routledge
Taylor & Francis Group

A PRODUCTIVITY PRESS BOOK

First published 2022
by Routledge
605 Third Avenue, New York, NY 10158

and by Routledge
2 Park Square, Milton Park, Abingdon, Oxon, OX14 4RN

Routledge is an imprint of the Taylor & Francis Group, an informa business

ISBN: 978-1-032-21060-5 (hbk)
ISBN: 978-1-032-21059-9 (pbk)
ISBN: 978-1-003-26655-6 (ebk)

DOI: 10.4324/9781003266556

Typeset in Garamond
by Apex CoVantage, LLC

MIX
Paper | Supporting responsible forestry
FSC
www.fsc.org
FSC™ C013985

Printed in the United Kingdom
by Henry Ling Limited

This book is dedicated
to my love,
my best friend,
my Power of One—
Kent.

Contents

About the Author

Recognized as a Top 30 Global Guru for Management, Natasha Bowman, JD, SPHR, has labored to transform the American workplace from the inside out for nearly 20 years. As a champion for employees, she's worked with a broad range of organizations as a C-suite human resources (HR) executive to create an engaging environment in which employees are respected, genuine leaders are cultivated, and top performance is achieved. Natasha is an award-winning, modern-day pioneer of workplace equality, inspiring organizations to not just pay lip service to workplace rights but to craft highly engaged cultures where *every* employee is truly dignified and valued for their contribution. Because of her ability to diagnose workplace issues and provide proven solutions to organizations, she is often referred to as the Workplace Doctor.

Natasha Bowman has developed a reputation as an expert workplace consultant through her firm, Performance ReNEW, and as a labor and employment law attorney. Her clients include 4A's, Hearst Magazines, Forbes, National Basketball Players Association, Google, McDonald's, and Manhattan College, to name a few. Apart from her rich expertise and cross-sector experience, she brings an ardent intellectual commitment to the field by serving as an adjunct professor of human resources for distinguished institutions such as Georgetown University, Fordham University, Manhattan College, and The Jack Welch Management Institute.

She is a sought-after TEDx and international keynote speaker for conferences and organizations worldwide and has shared her passion for creating positive and engaging workplaces by speaking at the HR Congress in Nice, France, New York Police Department, The City of Detroit, Ford Motor Company, The Employers' Association, Temple University, Harvard University, Toledo Public Schools, Microsoft, and the Society for Human Resources Management, just to name a few. Her expertise is frequently quoted in national publications such as *Forbes, Business Insider, U.S. News & World Report, Bloomberg BNA*, and *HR Magazine*.

Her bestselling book, *You Can't Do That at Work! 100 Legal Mistakes That Managers Make in the Workplace*, was published in 2017 and has been adopted as a critical resource for managers in organizations across America.

Introduction

It's 7 p.m. on a cool night in April. I've just walked out onto my porch with a pot in one hand and a wooden spoon in the other, and now I'm banging on that metal drum with all my might. What do the neighbors think? They're right there above and beside me—each one on his or her balcony making the same racket. Dogs are barking. Car alarms are going off. People are clapping and cheering. Tears begin to stream down my face as I lose my breath. You see, this isn't just any spring night in the Bronx. This is 2020, and I, along with all of my neighbors, are on lockdown due to COVID-19. The noise we're making is an act of solidarity—an acknowledgment that, although we can't be together in body, we're still together in spirit. Because of the thousands we're losing by the day to the virus in New York City and across the world, it's also a sign of mourning.

Just a month before that night on my balcony, I'd been planning my summer vacation, booking speaking engagements, seeing my daughter off to school, enjoying jazz clubs, and eating at nice restaurants with my husband—you know, doing what normal people do with their normal lives. I lived my life, much like everyone around me, without even a hint that those things wouldn't always be there and available for me to enjoy. But the spring of 2020 changed all that as travel was stopped, events were canceled, schools were closed, and businesses were shut down.

Especially in those early days, COVID-19 didn't just change our day-to-day lives; it also changed how we view the world and the people who truly impact it. We suddenly recognized and relied on all the people who we'd formerly paid little money and even less mind: service industry workers, law enforcement, firefighters, cashiers, food delivery personnel, postal workers, and so on. These people once worked in the background; now the invisible became visible: the invisible became essential. Although the rest of the world was at a standstill enjoying learning the latest TikTok dances, those now deemed essential kept the earth spinning by risking their lives to ensure we had what we needed in ours to survive.

I've been a workplace expert for more than 20 years. For much of that time, the perspective was that the real game-changers in life were the people who held fancy titles, commanded large salaries, and wore expensive suits. I strived to achieve that kind of influencer status, and through my teaching and writing, I tried to help others achieve that level of influence for themselves as well. But 2020 challenged that perception of superficial authority. In 2020 it was confirmed what we already should have known: the true game-changers in this world have no need for fancy titles or social or economic status. All that's needed is to cultivate personal power for the good of others—regardless of whether some organizational chart has given them the authority to do so—simple as that. This concept may seem a little too simple, but as you'll read in this book, the power that comes from cultivating civility, humanity, and equity in the workplace and beyond is not easy to obtain. It takes practice and commitment to improve both your lot and that of others.

A Young Girl and Her Broken Heart

When we talk about essential workers and the heroes of COVID-19, we can't help but think of healthcare workers.

Hour after hour, they stood on their feet with tight N95 masks on and saved one life after another. As hospitals in the country were forced to bar visitors from entering, these healthcare professionals sat with dying patients and held their hands until their last breath. They used their personal phones to facilitate visits via video chat. They brought people humanity and dignity in their darkest hours. Although the vast majority of these workers are small cogs in our nation's healthcare machine whose names we'll never know, they each became persons of massive influence in the lives they were able to touch. Collectively, they've inspired us all.

My appreciation for courageous healthcare professionals goes back much farther than COVID-19. When I was just a baby, my parents learned that I suffered from a congenital heart defect. For a decade, I was in and out of the hospital almost constantly. For some reason, I couldn't stop contracting pneumonia. It got so bad that, during the sixth grade, I spent more time in the hospital than out of it. My mother was certain the pneumonia was related to my heart condition. My cardiologist disagreed, refusing to make the connection between the two. As my health continued to deteriorate, my desperate mother resolved to hound the cardiologist's office daily until someone would have mercy on us. Every day, another disinterested nurse would refuse to hear her out.

One day, after a particularly long stint in the hospital, my mother called the cardiologist once more. This time, a new voice picked up the other line. She was a nurse like the countless others my mother had spoken to, but this nurse was different. She could hear the desperation in my mother's voice. Although she could have pushed us off as so many had before, she made a different choice. She decided to use the little power and influence she had to advocate on my behalf. Thanks to her, I finally got my chance to see the cardiologist after months of waiting. Lo and behold, at that long-awaited visit, it was determined that my pneumonia and heart defect were related. Go figure.

I wish I could say I left that appointment with a bottle of pills and a clean bill of health. Much the opposite, my parents and I sat dumbfounded as we heard the news: "without surgery, your little girl won't survive another six months." From there, everything was a whirlwind. It wasn't long before that cardiologist cut open my 11-year-old heart, repaired the defect, and set me on a path to a long, yet full recovery. We never would've gotten there, however, if it weren't for that one nurse. In a nutshell, the courage of one person to think and act outside of the status quo literally saved my life. That was the Power of One.

The Power of One

This book is about the potential you and I have to bring about extraordinary change in other people's lives. More than that, it's a way of life—a settled disposition to use our talents and skills to positively influence the people who inhabit our daily lives. This power isn't about positional authority based on our job title. It isn't the weight we throw around by virtue of our pedigree or the balance of our bank account. The Power of One is something we all have—whether you're a board-certified cardiologist or a vocational nurse. The question is, how will we use that power?

Too many of us operate in what I like to call default mode. Either we lean on our title as a source of superficial influence, or we cite our lack thereof as an excuse for powerlessness. In either case, we settle for a superficial notion of power that never cuts to the center of what we truly have to offer. "Powerful" executives use their stature to stand at an arm's-length from the real problems swirling around them. "Powerless" worker bees passively stand by and tolerate toxic and destructive behavior in the workplace. Either way, true power is never realized, influence is squandered, and real people get hurt in the process. I should know; I've seen it with my own eyes more times than I care to remember.

A Tale of Two Lawyers

The Power of One cuts both ways—positive and negative. Several years ago, for three years, I worked in a law firm in downtown Montgomery, Alabama. When I first walked in to fill the role of a temporary file clerk, I was simultaneously intrigued by the exquisite decor and deflated by the fact that I'd spend most of my days toiling away in the basement filing closed case files or pulling old ones. Three times a day, I'd head upstairs for 30 minutes to fill in for the receptionist while she took her smoke break.

About three months into my employment, one of the managing partners called me into her office. She was tiny yet bold, confident, and powerful. One of only two women attorneys at the firm, I'd frequently seen her go toe to toe with many of the men in the office without blinking an eye. Whenever she walked into a room, she commanded respect. I admired that woman more than words could say. When she spoke, I listened. So, when she said, "I need your help," you could imagine how surprised 24-year-old Natasha was. *My help? What could she possibly need from me?*

A few months before my arrival, the firm had lost its office manager, leaving this partner with far too much to handle on top of her regular caseload. Having seen my performance in the basement and at the front desk, plus knowing I was a recent grad, she decided I was exactly who she needed. Just like that, I was given a full-time job, a staff, and an office upstairs. As I laid in my bed that night and reflected on that conversation, I found a level of confidence I never knew I could have. Suddenly, I had hope—aspirations for a life that seemed so much bigger than I ever thought was available to me. Could I excel as an office manager? Could I go so far as to become an actual lawyer? I laid there and envisioned myself making six figures, wearing Dolce, and driving a fancy car to work. I even imagined the day when I could be the one to pull a 24-year-old woman up out of the basement and set her on a path to success. One conversation, endless possibilities. That's the Power of One.

For the next three years, I set out to master that job. As my responsibilities expanded, so did my aspirations. Instead of just longing for our attorneys' lot in life, I started plotting my way there. In 2004, I made a decent enough score on my LSAT to not only get into several law schools but to receive enough scholarship money to make the whole thing possible. When it came time for me to leave, the woman who hired me sent out a firm-wide email to mark my departure and celebrate my new journey. One by one, my fellow employees came to congratulate and wish me well. Later that day, how-ever, the only other African-American woman in our office came in to tell me how one of the partners had wished her good luck in law school. When she politely corrected him, the partner stared blankly: "So, who are you?" She'd been working there two years longer than I had, for a total of five years. That partner saw both of us every day, yet somehow, he thought we were the same person. Well, I knew the reason: we were simply the only two Black women in the office, and he simply didn't bother to distinguish us.

For all my other colleagues did to encourage me, this one man completely let the air out of my balloon. All of my excitement immediately vanished. Who was I to think I could become a high-profile, respected attorney in this field that was already so underrepresented by women and people of color? If I'd been invisible to him for three years, then how could I ever hope to gain anyone else's attention? That night, as I lay in my bed and considered the future, I had the exact opposite experience as I had three years before. My hope turned to fear.

My aspirations faded as my circumstances took on a whole new significance. Who was I to dare so greatly? Would I ever be respected? Would I ever be seen? Would I ever be heard? A single mom with no money in the bank, packing up to head to law school 10 hours from home. No family close by. No insurance. A car on its last leg. I should just stay here—in my place.

Conclusion: An Invitation to Power and Influence

What I didn't know at that time was how many people I would come across throughout my career with the same experience, the same feelings, and the same hopelessness. For a variety of reasons, many people feel undervalued. With a lack of voice in the workplace and despite their proven accomplishments, their career stagnates. Similar to how I felt that final day at the law firm, many would just lose their ambitions as they knew that no matter how high they reached, the bar continued to move higher.

I'm happy to say that I stayed the course and made it successfully through law school. But before I share the rest of my story, it's important we talk about where this book is heading. In the following pages, I want to invite you to join me on a journey toward personal power and intentional influence. As we go, we'll learn how to cultivate the Power of One through the three C's of influence: civility, candor, and courage. In Chapter 1, we begin by uncovering the dangers of the default mode and learning how to combat it. In Chapters 2–4, we take a closer look at each of the three C's, carefully defining each one, providing ample examples of what they look like in action, and following that up with practical steps to take toward becoming a person who wields the Power of One for the good of themselves and everyone they meet—at home, at work, and in the community.

As we get ready to move into Chapter 1, I want to ask you this question: who's had the most impactful influence on your life? Was it a well-known or glamorous celebrity that you only know through the lens of a TV screen or smartphone? Or was it an ordinary, day-to-day, unsung hero that no one knows beyond their circle? Now, let me ask you this: which one of those people would you call a leader? More importantly, which one of them would you rather be? If you're ready to become the kind of leader who inspires individuals and organizations to realize the power within themselves and move together toward greatness, then let's get started. The Power of One awaits!

Author's Note

The names, clients, companies, organizations, identifying details, and locations of my previous work experiences and former colleagues have been changed. These experiences are told from my perspective and from my memory of them.

Chapter 1

Asleep at the Wheel: The Dangers of the Default Mode

My husband was born and raised in Benton Harbor, Michigan. Located right on the shore of Lake Michigan, Benton Harbor was a popular destination for African-Americans who fled the South in the Great Northern Migration of the 1940s. In those days, the town's many automotive factories created an abundance of well-paying manufacturing jobs. As a result, these African-American families didn't just get to put food on the table, which was a very real struggle for them when they lived in the South. Better, they finally got to participate in the "American dream" of home ownership, a decent education, and a future full of limitless possibilities. In the late 1970s, however, outsourcing put a damper on all that. Eager to save a buck, manufacturers began to eliminate industrial jobs in Benton Harbor for cheaper labor in Mexico. Factories closed, jobs disappeared, and the pain of hopelessness quickly settled over this once-booming town.

DOI: 10.4324/9781003266556-1

It wasn't long before the crack epidemic spread to Benton Harbor. In the midst of the town's despair, drugs offered a sense of escape. For those men who'd lost their jobs, drugs also provided a means of providing for their families. What the men gained in terms of being breadwinners, however, these families quickly lost to poverty and despair. This hopelessness made it challenging for Black families to stay together. Thankfully, my husband was one of the lucky ones. Although his father had been a victim of Benton Harbor's sudden economic downturn, he managed to keep his seven children fed by refurbishing and selling vacuum cleaners out of his basement. It wasn't easy growing up with nine people in a two-bedroom home, but the Bowman household was filled with love, respect, and dignity.

Even so, parents can only do so much to help their kids withstand a tempest of negative influences outside of the home. I'm glad to say my husband's parents found a significant ally in his third-grade teacher. She knew how vulnerable her students were, and she made it her mission to keep them off the slippery slope toward despair and on the path to hope. Each morning, she'd begin class with a song:

> *Oh, what a beautiful morning,*
> *oh, what a beautiful day,*
> *oh, what a beautiful morning,*
> *nothing will stand in my way.*

What a way that was to start the day! From there, every lesson was fun and engaging. Her classroom was always a positive environment. Even if these kids didn't feel loved at home, they sure felt it at school. They mattered and they knew it. The Power of One.

Sadly, my husband's fourth-grade experience was the polar opposite. His new teacher looked out at his class of almost all African-American boys and immediately assumed the worst. They were nothing like the "good" (a.k.a. "white") kids over in St. Joseph. Instead, he thought they were destined to roam the streets of Benton Harbor, and he told them so. What was once a positive environment of respect and encouragement quickly devolved into a bitter clash of insults and bad attitudes. Instead of singing "Oh, what a beautiful morning," my husband and his classmates sulked into the classroom, ready to live down to their teacher's expectations. Where there had been A's and B's the year before, there were now C's and D's in their place. Innocence turned to deviance as these kids learned to hate school rather than to cherish it. Pride gave way to despair as they learned the "truth" about how short they fell and why they would never amount to anything in life. And the prophetic word their teacher spoke over those kids ultimately came true when a great many of them began to take on self-doubting, low self-esteem attitude, and a feeling of not being "enough" to pursue their goals and dreams.

Stuck in Default

Just like my childhood cardiologist and that discouraging partner at my first firm, my husband's fourth-grade teacher operated in what I call the *default mode*—a habitual descent into functional powerlessness. The default mode is . . .

- *habitual* in that it reflects a settled pattern of behavior. My uber-educated cardiologist had developed the habit of only relying on what he already knew and not seeking and exploring ideas and information.
- a *descent* in that we allow our biases and stereotypes to admit only a singular perspective of others. Instead of seeing his classroom as a field of rich possibility, my husband's fourth-grade teacher decided his energy would be

wasted on a group of African-American kids who could
have just one possible outcome.

■ *functionally powerless* in that it strips us of the resources
we already have. That cardiologist *silenced my mother.*
That partner *could've* seen me. That teacher *could've*
believed in a classroom full of Black kids. Regrettably,
due to the default mode, they *didn't* exercise their power,
which is the same as not having any to begin with.

Thankfully, my husband and I turned out alright. As stories
coming out of the #MeToo movement show, others haven't
been so lucky. One of the stories that strikes home for me is
that of a woman named Maria Diaz. Maria was a loving wife
and doting mother of three little girls. For the earliest years of
their lives, she poured herself out for them as a stay-at-home
mom. When her youngest was finally old enough for kinder-
garten, though, Maria decided to pursue her lifelong dream of
becoming a certified public accountant. She went to college
during the day, took care of her family in the evenings, and
studied well into the late-night hours. After four long years,
Maria completed her degree and became the first college
graduate from her family.

Academic success looked good on Maria, and corporate
America was quick to notice. Straight out of school, she signed
on to work for a big four accounting firm. Coming from a
family that discouraged women from entering the workforce,
Maria refused to take the opportunity for granted. She knew
she was on the leading edge of an entirely new future for her
and her three girls. But when Maria got to work, all her pride
and anticipation quickly began to fade. Maria's new boss didn't
want a thing to do with her. In fact, he barely said a word
to her. An email was his preferred mode of communication:
short, impersonal, to-the-point. That was fine, she supposed.
That's just how some people choose to communicate. But one
day, when Maria made the kind of mistake you'd expect from

a new accountant, all that changed. Rather than correct her in a simple email, Maria's boss chose to berate her in front of the entire office.

Crushed and humiliated, Maria pressed on nonetheless. Not long after, she began to notice the mood in her office. She'd come in expecting a culture of hard work and individual merit. Instead, she found an atmosphere of backstabbing, sabotage, and incivility. Everyone wanted to be a partner, and they were willing to do *anything* to get ahead. It wasn't long before Maria learned what it would take for *her* to climb the ladder. Pressured to attend an after-hours company event, she was quickly disgusted to see what happens when you add booze to an already toxic workplace culture. Worst of all, she encountered a pervasively sexual environment. Coworkers and senior leaders—even her own boss—all engaged in conversation that seemed entirely inappropriate for a professional setting. She was mortified by the sexual jokes, innuendo, and suggestive comments. Surely, she wasn't the only one made uncomfortable by this type of conversation and behavior, but the default mode has a nasty tendency of rendering good people silent in the face of what they'd otherwise be quick to condemn.

For the next year, the cycle continued. Passive-aggressive behavior from her boss, antagonistic relationships between coworkers, sexually charged encounters after work—all things that Maria felt uncomfortable with but endured for the sake of her career. Of course, all of the sexual tension had to express itself somewhere. And that's precisely what happened when, one night, her boss had a few too many drinks and decided to make his move. Pulling her aside, he went in for a kiss. Mortified, Maria got herself out of there and headed straight home to her husband. She trembled as she recounted the event. Embarrassed and ashamed, Maria struggled to share the intense burden she'd been forced to carry all this time. Her husband was livid but supportive.

Maria's husband encouraged her to report the incident, but she hesitated. That whole night she laid in bed thinking about all that might happen to her if she pressed the issue. Would they believe her? Would she lose her job? Would this ruin her reputation? After a while, though, she remembered her firm's "zero tolerance" policy for sexual harassment. If you thought you'd been a victim, it was your job to report it. No hesitation. So, the next morning, she mustered up every last ounce of courage and marched down to human resources to report what had happened. Right away, Maria was shocked to find herself on the defense against a barrage of belittling questions:

■ Are you sure that's how it happened?
■ Is that really what he did?
■ Maybe it was just a joke.
■ You know he's a senior partner in the firm, right?
■ Do you really want me to file this report?

Everything she had feared was coming true. It turned out the organization's tolerance for harassment was considerably higher than "zero" when it came to the conduct of its "more valuable" members. Still, Maria forged ahead. For two excruciating weeks, she waited for the investigation to run its course. When she was finally brought into HR, she felt a sense of relief in knowing this would all be over soon.

Maria's relief soon turned to despair as the woman on the other side of the table began to speak. "Maria," she said, "we've concluded our investigation and were not able to corroborate what you've alleged. In fact, we've learned you're the problem here. You haven't been performing as well as you ought, and you're just not a team player. So, as you know, we have a 12-month probationary period, and you didn't make the cut. Today will be your last day." Maria was devastated. She cried all the way home, wondering how she would share the awful news with her family. When she did walk in the front door, though, she decided not to say much at all. "I have a headache," she whispered, as she discreetly headed into the bedroom with a bottle of wine and a handful of pain pills. The next morning, Maria Diaz—faithful wife, devoted mother—did not wake up.

Maria's overdose was ruled accidental. When her coworkers heard what happened, they were shocked. They didn't see any of the toxicity that contributed to her untimely demise. Instead, they saw a busy mother—overtired, overworked, and unable to handle the demands of a big four accounting firm. Rather than take stock of their own complicity in her death, they washed their hands clean and moved on. "Tragic," they said as they got back to work. Had they not been stuck in default, they may have thought a bit harder about the conditions that led to her death. One of them may have chosen to exercise his or her own power to stand up for Maria's memory and to ensure nothing like that ever happened again. Unfortunately, they didn't. Score another one for the default.

Wake Up and Drive

Maria's story represents one particularly egregious instance of the default mode at work in an organization. Backstabbing coworkers, an "untouchable" boss, and a complicit human resources department—each of these actors chose to perpetuate the status quo rather than own up to their power and use it to serve others instead of themselves. Although the results may be less dramatic and pointed than what we saw with Maria, and the actors may be less overtly pernicious, the same default-mode thinking and citing exist in virtually every workplace—at least, every workplace I've been called to work with. This leads to all kinds of cultural pain, such as:

■ **Burnout.** Unchallenged assumptions about the correlation between working long hours and our personal commitment to the organization lead employees to overwork themselves.

■ **Homogeneity.** Organizational norms become a straitjacket as people are forced to conform rather than express their creative individuality.

■ **Fear.** Unchecked misbehavior on the part of superiors and high performers creates a reluctance to report for fear of retaliation. Bystanders and witnesses to misconduct duck under a "better them than me" mentality in order to survive.

As we saw with Maria, this last pain is the most destructive consequence of the default mode, and it's worth dwelling on a moment longer. When unchecked harmful behavior works its way through an organization, this behavior becomes a part of its culture. In Maria's case, the company had a *stated* culture in which there was to be "zero tolerance" for harassment and discrimination. In this, they aligned with virtually every other corporate entity in America and, more significantly, federal employment law. Yet, for Maria and untold numbers of women in corporate America, stated culture exists only on paper. The *actual* cultural environment in which they work not only tolerates harassment and discrimination, but it fosters it. I've watched high-performing CEOs get away with making a pass at every desirable object of the opposite sex. I've seen high performers get the benefit of the doubt even in the face of overwhelming evidence against them. Every time this happens, culture withers as employees learn what the organization is *actually* about.

An organization can post the laws and write up all the policies and regulations they want, but none of that will work to end harassment, discrimination, and all the other behavioral pains that rot companies from the inside out. Why? Because policy doesn't shape culture. Behavior shapes culture. Defined *and enforced* expectations shape culture. Accountability shapes culture. A policy isn't worth the paper it's written on if leadership isn't willing to demand conformity to the expectations set therein. Cultures only get changed when leaders recognize the default at work and get proactive and intentional about helping their employees cultivate the power to make a better place for themselves and their coworkers. As I'll argue in Chapter 4, we need environments marked by civility, courage, and candor if we're going to disengage the toxic behavior that threatens our organizations and re-engage the employees around or under us. And the only way we'll see that sort of cultural change is if we own our power and encourage others to do so as well. You may think that effecting such a shift is beyond your power, but change comes fast and hard when individual behaviors create a cycle of action.

What does that look like? A few years ago, I was invited to speak in the Middle East. My husband and I were nervous; all we knew of the region was what we saw in the media. We feared for our safety, doubting whether we could stay on the right side of what we perceived to be very strict cultural norms. Once we got there, though, we quickly realized our fears were unfounded. The people could not have been nicer, so much so that we had to come home and tell everyone how wrong we were. When we did, we inspired others to visit as well. Then they came home and did the same. Before long, we'd effected a cultural shift in our entire social network that pushed back against our default-mode thinking toward people from the Middle East. All it takes is one small push to set a cascade of dominoes in motion toward real cultural change.

Conclusion

Unless we snap out of the default mode and learn to harness the Power of One for ourselves and for our teams, we'll never be able to drive our organizations where they need to go. Whoever you are—whether you're a top-level executive or a ground-floor mechanic—today is the day to wake up and sing, "Oh, what a beautiful morning." We can no longer afford to passively trudge along in default while the world passes us by. Instead, we need to begin shaping our reality and wielding the power we have to create the change we want to see in ourselves and others. Whoever you are, wherever you are, you have the power to break out of the default mode and make the world better for you and everyone else in it. Not convinced? Keep reading.

Chapter 2

The Power You Don't Think You Have

In the last chapter, we considered the default mode and the dangers of ignoring the power we all have to effect change. Right away, I want to anticipate a common objection: "Natasha, I don't have the power you think I have." I know the objection because I've heard it so many times on the lips of people who've learned to equate power with a job title or position of power. I've heard it from recent college graduates who clearly see the dysfunction in their new companies yet don't think they've put in enough time to instigate positive change. I've also heard it from seasoned veterans who haven't made it all that far up the ladder and are fed up with their perceived lack of influence and authority.

In this chapter, we're going to talk about real power—the kind of potential that belongs to people we'd traditionally write off as "powerless." Of course, there's no shortage of people like these who've gone on to effect massive change in their lives and the world around them: Rosa Parks, Mother Teresa, Malala Yousafzai, Mahatma Gandhi. But here I want to share a lesser-known name: Harold Cottam.

DOI: 10.4324/9781003266556-2

Cottam was a wireless operator on the *Carpathia*—a British passenger ship operating in the Atlantic Ocean in the early 20th century. On the night of April 14, 1912, Cottam left his wireless earpiece in as he prepared for bed. That wasn't common practice, but he was expecting a transmission from another ship. What he received, though, was a distress call from Jack Phillips, the wireless officer aboard the world's largest and most popular new ship: *Titanic*. The unsinkable ship had struck an iceberg and, though other vessels were much closer than the *Carpathia*, Cottam's earpiece was the only one to receive the ship's messages of distress.

Immediately, Cottam reported the distress call to First Officer Horace Dean. Dean was unconvinced that the *Titanic* was actually in trouble and refused to wake the ship's captain, Arthur Rostron. Cottam, unable to bear with Dean's disbelief, broke protocol, overstepped his chain of command, and rushed down to Rostron's cabin. Right away, the captain gave the order to turn *Carpathia* around and make full steam toward the sinking *Titanic*—a four-hour journey for the little ship. They arrived at the scene about an hour and a half after the *Titanic* sank—five hours before anyone else. In all, *Carpathia* and her crew were able to rescue 705 passengers from 20 lifeboats. If they hadn't been there, there's no telling how many of those people would've survived—if any.

In his testimony before the U.S. Senate, Rostron described the whole situation as

> absolutely providential . . . the wireless operator was
> in his cabin, at the time, not on official business
> at all, but just simply listening as he was undress-
> ing. . . . In 10 minutes, maybe he would have been
> in bed, and we would not have heard the messages.[1]

What he didn't highlight, though, was Cottam's decision to buck the chain of command in order to get the message past Dean and into the captain's ears. In a split second, the "powerless" wireless operator's decision to step over the "powerful" First Officer resulted in the rescue of more than 700 passengers.

Do You Have the Power?

Something about Cottam's story resonates deeply with us all. We love the romance of it—the idea of the virtuous underdog overcoming complacency to serve the greater good. Cottam is like a modern-day David, encouraging us all to conquer whatever Goliath stands between us and what we know is right. But when it comes to our everyday lives, most of us are simply too afraid to grab our five smooth stones and face the giant. Like Maria Diaz's silent coworkers, we get stuck in the default, tricking ourselves into thinking we're powerless to effect change in our circumstances. Why?

For some, the problem is a lack of confidence. In both our professional and personal lives, we often make excuses for why we're not achieving our full potential. We amplify the negativity of others and accept the barriers they've placed before us. Worse, we erect barriers of our own and neglect all the professional and psychological resources that exist to help us overcome our limits and pursue new levels of power and excellence. We convince ourselves of our weakness and learn to live as though we have no power. Call it the powerlessness of none—the idea that we've got absolutely nothing to offer.

Shaquem Griffin grew up with every reason to doubt his power. Born with a rare complication that prevented his left hand from forming properly, Griffin's early years were marked by unyielding pain. At the age of four, his parents made the dreadfully difficult decision to amputate his hand. Still, Griffin went on to excel in sports, eventually earning a spot on the University of Central Florida's football team. I remember watching Griffin play during the 2017 college football season. My husband and I stared at the screen in amazement as Griffin led his team to an undefeated season. Two years prior, the team had lost every one of their games. But, with Griffin on the field, the Knights were on fire. He stripped balls, intercepted passes, sacked quarterbacks, recovered fumbles—all the stuff you'd expect from a star line-backer. All of it, of course, with only one hand.

Shaquem—now a linebacker for the Seattle Seahawks alongside his twin brother, Shaquill—is the poster child for finding your own power. He never bought into the negativity. He refused to believe that his lack of a left hand rendered him powerless. Instead, he used his one hand to accomplish more than most players could with two. He used the power *he* had to lead his team to victory and became an inspiration for people all over the world—athlete or not. Griffin was once quoted as saying, "You're not disabled unless you say you're disabled." To paraphrase that idea, you're not powerless unless you say and believe you're powerless.

A Distinction That Makes All the Difference

Sometimes, our perceived powerlessness is less about a lack of confidence and more about a lack of external authority. We feel like we can make a difference, but we haven't been given the formal permission to do so. At a certain level, that makes sense. From the day we were born, we learned to admire and respect titles. Little girls like me were taught to look forward to the day when Prince Charming would show up and sweep us off our feet. For little boys, Superman was the one who'd come to the rescue. We were powerless; they were powerful. We were the ones in need of saving; they were the saviors.

We grew up, of course, and learned to stop looking off into the horizon and start looking up the organizational chart instead. *Real* power, we discovered, has nothing to do with a white horse or a red cape. Rather, it has to do with connections and credentials. The lesson many of us have had drilled into our heads is that, unless you climb the ladder into a position of authority, the only power you have is the power your superiors *say* you can have. "I better stay in my lane," we've learned to tell ourselves. "If I don't, I'll ruffle the wrong feathers and find myself put out of a job."

Make no mistake; job titles bring a certain level of power. President of the United States is the most powerful title in the entire world from the perspective of legal authority and military might. Chief Executive Officer (CEO) is the most powerful title in an organization with respect to operations, execution, and vision. But what about the power of influence? Plenty of presidents have slinked into obscurity once their terms were up, all because they failed to truly influence the masses. CEOs come and go; only a precious few leave a true and lasting legacy. People like these wield power over many, but their power only runs skin deep. As soon as they fade, it fades.

Power is about more than raw authority or professional privilege. Think about it; who has more influence over an individual community? The president, or the beloved local mayor? Who has more sway over you at work? The boss at the top of the ladder, or someone much farther down such as an immediate supervisor who started at the bottom but remembers what it's like to be on the front lines? Or maybe it's the colleague who works double shifts and raises three kids alone but still shows up to work with a smile and a positive attitude. When we look at the people who have the deepest and longest-lasting impact on our lives, they're very often not the ones who wield the most organizational power over us.

All this leads us to the fact that, when we think about the relationships between title and power, we have to distinguish between two types of power or authority: **positional** and **dispositional**. Positional authority is the kind of power that comes with a job title. The positional authority says "Jump!" and you jump dutifully, not because you respect and admire

her but because you've got kids to feed. Dispositional authority, on the other hand, is power that comes from relationships
of trust and respect. The dispositional authority says "Jump!"
and you do it cheerfully, all because you *know* she's got a
good reason, and you *trust* that she's got your and your company's best interest at heart.

Positional authorities carry the power of the sword; they can
nix your organizational existence in an instant. They hold your
livelihood in their hands and use that power to accomplish
their ends. Sometimes, they do it in an evil, vindictive way—
much like we saw with Maria in the previous chapter. Most of
the time, though, these positional authorities are much less sin-
ister. Leaders who operate in the default mode can be kind, yet
clueless. They lead from a place of positional authority simply
because they haven't done the hard relational work it takes to
cultivate dispositional power. Thanks to their job titles, they've
never really had to. As a result, they see the world in terms of
carrots and sticks, and they create a dynamic in which people
are motivated more by personal interest than by a genuine
desire to benefit one another and the team.

Ideally, leaders with titles would exercise *both* types of
power. In healthy organizations, those employees who've
cultivated the most dispositional authority get to climb the
ranks and run the company. Unfortunately, that isn't always (or
often!) the case. Instead, you find employees with a great deal
of dispositional power strewn throughout the organization at
every level. Like Harold Cottam, these people find ways to
circumvent the normal flow of power and exert real influence
from where they are. They're the middle manager who sacrifices her own corporate well-being for the sake of her direct
reports. They're the assembly-line worker who lobbies management to improve working conditions for his fellow workers.
Yes, they're even the executive who goes out of her way to
spend time with, encourage, and find creative ways to advance
the marginalized members of her organization.

During my tenure as a human resources executive in the healthcare industry, I learned firsthand how important it is to marry both positional and dispositional power. As Chief Negotiator, I was charged with mediating a historically contentious relationship between a hospital and its labor union. As you could imagine, negotiations such as these typically drag on as each side digs in their heels against the other. When I started, the union leaders on the other side of the table saw me as your typical "suit" called in to stick *up* for the hospital while sticking it *to* the people who staffed it. And who could blame them? My predecessor had been precisely what they were most afraid of—a corporate functionary with a track record of strong-arm tactics and one-sided deals. Why should they expect me to be any different?

For a year, I made it my mission to prove those union members wrong. I wanted to show them that I had no intention of using my position as an opportunity to bully them into submission. My positional power gave me the authority to make decisions that benefited *both* the hospital and its staff—not to fleece the latter for the sake of the former. When I used that power intentionally, it earned me dispositional authority with our skeptical union members. When I made it a point to acknowledge the hospital's missteps and own its failure, those little acts of civility only strengthened my budding relationships with the union.

As a result of this time and effort spent developing dispositional authority, when it came time to negotiate, the decision-makers in the room knew I was being 100% genuine when I opened our session with the following: "Both sides of the table are here to ensure that every employee feels valued, are fairly compensated, and know that they are part of something bigger than all of us." Four short hours (not months) later, we all walked away feeling like we'd won something—all because of the synergy that happens when we stop leaning on positional power and start intentionally cultivating its dispositional complement.

The Power of One is another name for this dispositional power. It's the power we all carry with us irrespective of our job title or socioeconomic status. The Power of One is strategic and pragmatic; it's not a delusion of grandeur so much as an honest assessment of who we are, where we are, and what we bring to the table. It refuses to listen to negativity—either from within or without. Instead, it owns the moment and leans into the present with all the resources at its disposal. More than that, it commits to positive action. It says, "No matter where I am or what my official role may be, I'm going to cultivate my power and seek ways to express it for the good of myself and the people around me."

The Power of One trusts that positional authority will follow from the competence shown and confidence earned through dispositional power. Still, even if that positional authority never comes, it resolves to never quit asserting itself. The Power of One loves the encouragement of others, but it refuses to bow down to any voice but its own. Like Harold Cottam, it tramples the First Officer when it has to in order to serve the greater good.

Conclusion

Throughout this chapter, we've seen vivid examples of what can happen when we refuse to admit our powerlessness and, instead, take up the Power of One. One of my favorite stories of this power at work in history comes from the middle of the 19th century, when slavery was widespread in the South yet virtually unacknowledged in the North. During this time of injustice and apathy, Harriet Beecher Stowe and her family actively helped enslaved Africans escape slavery through the underground railroad. But that wasn't enough for her. She wanted to end slavery. Stowe was not an elected official. She did not have great wealth. She did not hold a position of power or influence. As a woman living in the 1800s, she did not even have the right to vote! So, she used the only power she had—her pen. A series of stories that eventually became a book, Stowe's *Uncle Tom's Cabin* awakened the nation to the cruelty of slavery and prompted thousands to join and fund the abolitionist movement. Her book has been cited as one of the primary factors that sparked the Civil War. She was proactive and intentional in her pursuit for the greater good. It's rumored that when Harriet Beecher Stowe met President Abraham Lincoln, he said to her, "So you're the little lady that started this Great War."

Stowe's unshakable drive to use any means at her disposal to break down inhumanity and cultivate a safe and inclusive space for all—this is what lies at the heart of the Power of One. How do we cultivate that power? That's a question I intend to spend the rest of this book answering. But, before I do, allow me this one last example to show how crucial it is that we acknowledge our power and begin to actively cultivate it. Imagine I hand you a suitcase filled with $1 million in cash—no strings attached, you can spend it wherever and however you want. Now, imagine you take that suitcase home, stuff it in your closet, and go on about your life as if nothing ever happened. Take it a step further and imagine you lose your job, fall behind on your mortgage, let your electricity bill slide, and stop putting food on your table. All the while, that suitcase full of cash is just sitting in your closet collecting dust. Everything you need to escape from your current situation is in that suitcase, but you just won't go in there and grab it.

Sounds ridiculous, doesn't it? Of course, you'd go into the closet and pull out the resources you need to change your life for the better. Well, we've all got that metaphorical suitcase in our closet. Most of us are holding on to an untapped cache of resources greater than anything we could ever imagine for ourselves. Our suitcase is full, but we refuse to go into the closet and crack it open. Instead of spending our power that comes in abundance, we're leaving it to collect dust. Why? Because no one has given us permission to open the case? Well, who gets to make *that* call? Or have we convinced our-selves the suitcase doesn't even exist? Either way, the result is the same: the powerlessness of none.

It's time we dragged the suitcase out of the closet, opened it, and started spending our power on the people and things that matter most. But what shape should that take? How do we spend our power in a way that's wise and helpful? To that question, we now turn.

Note

1. United States Senate Inquiry, Day 1, Testimony of Arthur H. Rostron. "Titanic" disaster, report of the Committee on Commerce, United States Senate, April 19, 1012, pursuant to S. Res. 283, directing the committee on commerce to inves-tigate the causes leading to the wreck of the White Star liner "Titanic," accessed October 5, 2021.

Chapter 3

For Such a Time as This

The biblical book of Esther tells the story of a young woman stolen from her ancestral people and forced to become a queen. When a wicked advisor conspires to destroy her people, Esther's Uncle Mordecai appears with a plea that she uses her power to influence the king and save the Jews from destruction. At first, she refuses. Approaching the king without an invitation would place her own life in jeopardy. But Mordecai reminds Esther that her and her entire family's fate will be tied to that of the Jews regardless of whether she intervenes or not. Then, he forces her to reckon with the great responsibility her position of influence has afforded her, "And who knows whether you have not come to the kingdom for such a time as this?"[1] At this, Esther changes her mind and enacts a plan that would eventually bring down the wicked advisor and deliver the Jews from danger.

Many in our culture are dealing with their own "Esther" moment right now. Massive social movements centered around workplace equality, racial justice, and criminal justice reform have awakened our society to the plight of the less privileged among us. Like a million little Mordecais, the videos and images we've seen plastered across social media each bring

DOI: 10.4324/9781003266556-3

with them a vivid plea. Will we use whatever power and privilege we have to come to the aid of the marginalized in our society? Will we risk our own status and reputation in order to lend a voice to the voiceless? Will we set aside our blissful ignorance and overcome our penchant for self-preservation so that we can elevate those who've been held down? In a word, will we become allies?

Something Better Than an Ally

One of the most encouraging aspects of the past several years has been the number of Americans who are willing to stand up for their coworkers, friends, and neighbors by becoming allies in the fight against injustice. Writing in *Harvard Business Review*, Tsedale M. Melaku, Angie Beeman, David G. Smith, and W. Brad Johnson describe allyship as "a *strategic* mechanism used by individuals to become *collaborators*, *accomplices*, and *coconspirators* who fight injustice and promote equity in the workplace through supportive personal relationships and public acts of sponsorship and advocacy."[2] Allies, in other words, seek out ways to empower their disempowered neighbors.

Allyship is a beautiful thing for which I am immensely grateful, but I think it only brings us partway toward the equal future we desire. For one thing, one of the struggles reported by people of color in the workplace is "performative allyship." Although virtually every company in America has signaled its virtuous desire to promote equal treatment for all, too many of these self-professed allies continue to undermine equality by underpaying or holding back women and people of color.[3] Even when allies do their best to walk in step with their professed desire to level the field and combat injustice, a significant gap exists between action and perception. According to a study on allyship in the workplace from LeanIn.org, more than

80% of white men and women see themselves as allies, yet only 45% of Black women and 55% of Latinas think they have such allies at work.[4] What gives?

I'm not out to critique allyship, but even when it's done well, it takes the lines that divide us for granted. In seeking to heal the divisions, it perpetuates them by failing to strike at the root of the problem: an us vs. them mentality. That mentality is evident in the gap mentioned above, and it inevitably creates the perception that intolerance, discrimination, and harassment are "their" problem and that "we're" going to solve it for them. From this perspective, the ally is a supporter from without rather than a collaborator within. *We* help *them* to become more like we are, as opposed to *us* working together to lift the entire organization to a new level. We may be *for* them, but we're never truly *with* them. So, while allyship is a wonderful phenomenon, I don't think it's enough to bring us together. For that, we need something more.

From Allyship to Ourship

To illustrate that "something more," let me tell you about an unlikely hero from Waco, Texas.[5] Born on October 12, 1919, Doris Miller was the son of sharecroppers and the grandson of enslaved Africans. Twenty years later, he joined the Navy as a Mess Attendant Third Class. His duties revolved around cooking, cleaning, and doing the laundry. That was about all the responsibility the highly segregated U.S. military was willing to entrust into the hands of a Black man at that time. But all of that changed on December 7, 1941, when the "date which will live in infamy" also became the day when Miller showed the world just what a Black man can do in the service of his country.

Miller was collecting laundry below deck when a Japanese torpedo struck his ship, the *West Virginia*. Miller immediately reported to his battle station, only to discover that it had been destroyed. Scrambling his way above deck, the sailor was assigned to help carry the wounded to shelter as the Japanese attack raged around him. In the midst of the chaos, Miller was eventually ordered to man a .50-caliber Browning machine gun—a weapon with which he had absolutely no training. When the ammo was spent, Miller made his way to the boat deck, pulling wounded sailors from the flaming waters. After the order to abandon ship was given, Miller swam nearly 400 yards, narrowly avoiding enemy gunfire. When he got to shore, he stayed to help injured sailors instead of running for cover.

Miller was eventually awarded the Navy Cross for his heroism. He became a national icon for civil rights and equal treatment in the military before perishing in a Japanese submarine attack on November 24, 1943. His story is just one brilliant example of the countless Black men who jumped into the fray of World War II. These heroes willingly took up arms to defend an ideal of life, liberty, and justice that they had not yet experienced in America and were unlikely to enjoy even if they did win the war. Why? Because when the bombs were dropping in Pearl Harbor, brave men like Doris Miller said to themselves, "We're in this together. This is not *their* problem; it's *ours*. This is not *their* ship; it's *our* ship."

Ourship. That's precisely the concept we need in order to take allyship to the next level. Ourship is about more than sympathy—observing the plight of others without personally entering into it with them. But it's also about more than empathy—imagining what it feels like to be in someone else's shoes. Ourship begins with sympathy and empathy, but it culminates in our entering the fray and suffering *together* with those who've been marginalized. Ourship is not opposed to allyship. Instead, the former perfects the latter as it encourages allies not just to strategize but to *lay down* their privilege and power for the sake of others. Ourship is not just about standing *by* them; it's about standing *with* them. It's about seeing *their* problems as *our* problems and using or giving away our Power of One to help others realize their own.

Consider two amazing women who used their power to advocate on behalf of the marginalized: Princess Diana and Mother Teresa. Diana was the ally *par excellence*. She traveled the world, confronting despair so that she could give a voice to the voiceless. Still, she could always retreat into the safety of her own privilege. The problems she faced always remained outside of and, therefore, apart from her. Teresa, on the other hand, entered fully into the suffering she sought to allay. She took a vow of poverty and joined herself intimately to the poorest of the poor. She divested herself of all her power and privilege to throw in her lot with the people she desired to help. She embodied ourship by making their problem her own. I have nothing but respect for *both* of these women, but I can't help but think that Teresa's work will have a deeper and longer-lasting impact among the people of Calcutta, as well as the millions of people around the globe who were influenced by her example.

In the corporate sphere, the most encouraging displays of ourship I've seen have come from those leaders who decided to lay aside their own power and privilege to elevate minority leaders to power. For example, founder and former CEO of Reddit, Alexis Ohanian, chose to give up his seat on the board of the social news aggregator to specifically make room for a person of color.[6] He also vowed to contribute future gains from his company's stock to investment in the Black community. Ohanian's seat on the board was taken by its first Black member, Michael Seibel, who rose to Silicon Valley notoriety by co-founding the popular streaming platform Twitch (formerly, Justin.tv) and going on to become CEO of the influential startup incubator Y Combinator.

Although ourship won't always mean giving up your seat at the table, the willingness to make that sacrifice for the sake of others is precisely what I'm talking about. Ohaninan recognized that if both his company and our country were to make forward progress, it would require sacrificial leadership: "I believe resignation can actually be an act of leadership from people in power right now. . . . To everyone fighting to fix our broken nation: do not stop."[7] In other words, it would involve both the recognition of his Power of One and the willingness to spend it for the sake of others.

Owning and Spending Your Power

The purpose of this entire book is to help you own your Power of One and spend it in ways that empower others to own theirs, as well. But the needs in our society are too urgent to put off until you've had a chance to finish this book. That said, here are three ways you can begin practicing ourship today:

Own your power. What do you already have at your disposal? Are you in a position of leadership at work or in the community? Do you have the authority to rewrite and/ or enforce policy? Are you an influencer?

Uncover the powerless. Who are the marginalized around you? How does their lack of power keep them down? Ask what they're lacking and consider what forces are at work in holding them back. Identify where you can join in their distress and empower them to move forward.

Relentlessly persevere. If you make others' problems your own and if you deliberately share your power, you will find yourself suffering alongside them. Don't give up; this is very much the point of ourship. In this community of suffering, we're forced to work together to make a better place for *everyone*. Don't give up on the way to that crucial goal.

Conclusion

In the 1940s' U.S. Navy, Doris Miller had no institutional power to speak of; the only power he had was the physical strength he used to man his ship's guns and bear his fellow

Doris Miller pinned with Navy Cross.

Photo: U.S. Navy

sailors to safety. The thing that saved his life and the lives of so many others that day wasn't a calculated decision to become allies with the weak and wounded around him. There was no time for that; the situation was far too urgent. Instead of looking around for allies, he saw his shipmates not as black and white, but as fellow human beings. Their suffering was his suffering. Their problem was his problem. Their ship was his ship. Ourship.

If you're reading this book, then you likely have far more power than Miller ever had. I dedicated Chapter 2 to convincing you of that, and I plan to keep banging that same drum from here on out as we think about how best to own and spend power for the sake of our organizations, communities, and homes. For now, remember that there are people around you who don't just need your power; they need *you*. They need you to get down into the muck with them, not just as allies who get to go home when things get nasty. They need you to lock arms with them and channel your best Esther or Doris Miller to say, "This is our problem, and we've been given our power for such a time as this. Let's use it to save our ship."

Notes

1. *The Holy Bible: English Standard Version* (Wheaton, IL: Crossway Bibles, 2016), Es 4:13–14.
2. Tsedale M. Melaku, Angie Beeman, David G. Smith, and W. Brad Johnson, "Be a Better Ally," *Harvard Business Review*, November–December 2020.
3. Karen Yuan, "Black Employees Say 'Performative Allyship' is an Unchecked Problem in the Office," *Fortune.com Magazine*, June 19, 2020.
4. "White Employees see Themselves as Allies—But Black Women and Latinas Disagree," *Lean In*, accessed October 5, 2021 from https://leanin.org/research/allyship-at-work.

5. Thomas W. Cutrer and T. Michael Parrish, "How Navy Hero Dorie Miller's Bravery Helped Fight Discrimination in the U.S. Military," *HistoryNet*, December 2019, accessed October 5, 2021 from www.historynet.com/beyond-the-call-of-duty.htm.

6. Taylor Hatmaker and Ingrid Lunden, "Alexis Ohanan Steps Down from Reddit Board, Asks for His Seat to Go to a Black Board Member," *Tech Crunch*, June 5, 2020, accessed October 5, 2021 at https://techcrunch.com/2020/06/05/alexis-ohanian-steps-down-reddit-board/.

7. Ibid.

Chapter 4

The Three C's of Influence

Meet Jane. Jane worked as a junior executive in marketing at WalTarget for the past five years. She wouldn't call herself a creative, but Jane oversees an in-house team of graphic designers and copywriters. Let's just say her left-brained sensibility consistently rubs her right-brained team members the wrong way. Always focused on strategy at the expense of creativity, Jane frequently shoots down her designers' attempts to think outside the box. Lately, her team has begun to stagnate. Their marketing campaigns lack energy, and Jane's analytic approach is turning into a real drag for everyone. Rather than take responsibility for the team's lackluster performance, though, she shifts the blame. If only the team would get on Jane's page, then their numbers would improve.

Meet Joe. Joe has worked at WalTarget for the same amount of time as Jane. He, too, is a junior marketing executive, and the team he leads is nearly identical to that of his colleague. Like Jane, Joe is a left-brained number-cruncher with an eye for strategy. Unlike his counterpart, Joe goes out of his way to receive and consider his subordinates' creative input with

DOI: 10.4324/9781003266556-4

civility. Instead of rejecting them out of hand, he embodies a sense of genuine *candor*—eager to debate every decision on the merits and never to let his words and actions fall out of sync with his thoughts and intentions. When his team wins, Joe is quick to share the praise. When they lose, he's got the *courage* to own the loss—letting the burden of failure fall on *his* back instead of passing it down the line.

Now that you've met Joe and Jane, let me ask you a few questions. Despite their identical positions, who do you think holds more power at WalTarget? Who do you think stands a better chance of moving up into a position of greater responsibility? Which set of employees do you think will perform better over the long haul? Who would *you* rather work for? In a word, which of these managers do you think has the power to *influence* his or her colleagues and team members for the better?

Influence and the Power of One

What is the Power of One? Is it the power to intimidate others into doing what we want them to do? Is it the power to cleverly manipulate people to our own ends? Or is it something else? Earlier in this book, we talked about *dispositional* power—the relational force that arises out of the deep well of personal resources we bring to our everyday lives. Still, what does that power *do*? How does it encounter the world around us, and what does that tell us about how we're supposed to cultivate the Power of One for our own good and the benefit of others?

Here's my simple answer to that question: the Power of One is the power of positive *influence*. If you break the word down into its Latin roots (*in* + *fluere*), *influence* literally means "to flow in." To say we've been influenced by someone or something is to say that we've allowed an idea or a sensibility to flow into our consciousness and affect the way we approach the world. I've been influenced by more people than I can count: my parents, the partner who gave me my first real opportunity in law, my husband. So have you. Each in their own way, people of influence have made us who we are today.

For there to have been an inflow toward us, of course, there had to be an outflow from elsewhere. In other words, the people who influenced us had to own their power and wield it for our good. I can point to plenty of people along the way who *didn't* wield their power for my good: the stubborn cardiologist, the racially obtuse law partner, and so on. Instead, they exercised a kind of dark power that both literally and figuratively could've ended my journey before it even started. Yet, I refuse to say they "influenced" me because whatever they hurled in my direction was most certainly not intended to add to or flow positively into my consciousness. Rather, it was a selfish attempt to *take* something by reducing me to little more than a name on a chart or a means to an end.

The Shape of Powerful Influence

What makes for real influence? What distinguishes the dark power of negativity from the enlightening force of positivity? We caught a hint of it above in my description of Joe and Jane. In that fictional scenario, Jane was an uncivil and duplicitous manager who lacked the nerve to own her shortcomings. Joe, on the other hand, consistently acted with **civility**, **candor**, and **courage** toward others. As I'll unpack at length throughout the rest of this book, these are the three C's of influence—the personal and professional virtues that enable us to cultivate *real* power in ourselves and use it for the good of others.

This is what the Power of One looks like: a human being who embraces and encourages others' humanity (civility), lives and speaks the truth no matter what the consequences (candor), and steps willingly into hardship or complexity rather than shrinking back from it (courage). By definition, the person who embodies these three virtues *will* influence the people around her for the better. Whether she finds herself at the top of the ladder or the bottom, the power she wields will be undeniable.

Before I introduce the three C's individually, it's important we realize something about the social reality of the Power of One. Contrary to what the name might imply, this power doesn't exist in isolation. It simply can't stay locked up in itself. Unexpressed power isn't power at all; it's mere potential. In the same way a battery needs a flashlight or ignition switch to actualize its chemical potential, the Power of One needs to make contact with others for it to truly come into its own. Because this power lives and moves toward others, it will always be a force for change. For that reason, we won't just focus on the individual benefits of power and influence but their cultural impact as well.

Civility: Human Beings in Corporate Space

Families, companies, neighborhood associations—these are the social circles that make up our civilized reality. For us to thrive in these basic units of society, we've got to get along with one another. A spat with your neighbor may put the block on ice. A disagreement with one of your peers at work may seriously compromise your ability to get the job done. For civilization to work at any level, we've got to learn how to be *civil*. Contrary to common opinion, civility isn't about weakness. To be "civil," you don't have to lay down and let others walk all over you. Instead, civility is a type of ownership. It says, "We're in this together," and it refuses to let individual friction sidetrack our collective mission.

At the broadest level, civility is about joining others in this common project we call human civilization. Opal Tometi, one of the co-founders of Black Lives Matter, defines it as "the recognition that all people have dignity that's inherent to their person, no matter their religion, race, gender, sexuality, or ability."[1] At its core, civility recognizes the inherent value of others and refuses to treat them in any way that would deny or rob them of their humanity. Civility goes out of its way to respect others—to offer them the same consideration one would wish to receive in return. It refuses to tear down or take shots. Instead, civility seeks to build up the other for the sake of their growth and the common good.

At the more local level, civility is about joining a smaller circle of others in common projects we call "the company" or "the neighborhood." It affirms our humanity and puts it in a specific context. A truly civil worker or volunteer wields his power, not for the sake of personal gain but for the greater good. Like Joe, he brings his unique skills to every project. Unlike Jane, he's willing to admit when his unique perspective has led him astray. Why? Because civility sets its sights on the good of the whole—not the advancement of one particular citizen. Civility recognizes our involvement in a common project, and it challenges individuals to take up their place within that shared space.

How does civility intersect with power? Does respecting others' inherent humanity and sacrificing our own interests for the greater good really translate to an *increase* in personal power? For too many "old school" leaders, the answer to that question is no. Power, they say, is gained at the expense of others. Bullies on the playground increase their power by stripping it from others. In the same way, corporate bullies learn to claw their way to the top by tearing down the people around them. Their view of power dynamics is zero-sum; it inevitably requires unhealthy competition, one-upmanship, and doing whatever it takes to get ahead.

If the recent progress we've seen in minimizing harassment and maximizing inclusion has shown us anything, it's that the power dynamics of corporate America are shifting dramatically. Although far too many bullies remain, the reality is that *civility* can do more to advance individual careers and bind companies together than the "I win; you lose" attitude that typifies so many approaches to power and influence. If you want to be the kind of person who influences others, the power to do that will never come at their expense. Paradoxically, it'll come at *your* expense as you spend what power you do have for the sake of the people around you and the common good. Consider it an investment that is guaranteed to provide an abundant return.

Candor: Getting Clear on What It Means to be Transparent

Following the scandalous demise of companies such as Enron and WorldCom, "transparency" has become a key buzzword in corporate America. The kind of transparency that truly counts, though, is about more than annual reports and Securities Exchange Commission filings. Rather, it strikes at the cultural core of an organization. As business professors James O'Toole and Warren Bennis have argued, "no organization can be honest with the public if it's not honest with itself."[2] Along those lines, O'Toole and Bennis define *transparency* as "the degree to which information flows freely within an organization, among managers and employees, and outward to stakeholders."[3] How do we create this type of transparency in our organizations? One word: candor.

What is candor? For our purposes, candor is the integrity of a person's speech, thoughts, and actions. A candid person is one who speaks the truth, approaches every issue fairmindedly, and does what she says she's going to do. Candor is a kind of holistic honesty that strips away our natural desire to obfuscate or tiptoe around the truth. To say someone has candor is to say you trust them to give it to you straight. Whether they're right or not, you don't have to worry about whether they're telling you what they believe to be the truth. You don't have to second-guess their motives or wonder whether they'll stab you in the back the moment you turn around. A candid coworker or boss creates psychological safety for you and your coworkers, not because they make you feel good all the time but because you always know where they stand. Therefore, you always know where *you* stand as well.

The value of candor is both personal and organizational. O'Toole and Bennis demonstrate the value of candor by focusing on a study conducted by NASA in the 1980s. The study, looking at the human factors that led to airline accidents, took already existing cockpit crews and placed them in a flight simulator to see how they would respond in crisis scenarios. What they found was that those pilots who tended to take charge in the moment were far more likely to make the wrong decision than those who first sought input from their crew.

The superficial lesson of this study is clear: don't make a decision until you gather all the facts. When organizational theorists took a deeper look at the study, however, they found that what happened in the flight simulator was more a product of the crew's prior working experience than what they said or did in that singular moment of crisis. In other words, it wasn't a matter of information in the moment but habituation over time—learned patterns of behavior that had been ingrained through hours of time together in the air. Candid pilots fostered candid cockpits: "The pilots who'd made the right choices routinely had open exchanges with their crew members."[4] On the flip side, closed-off pilots fostered closed-off cockpits: "crew members who had regularly worked with the 'decisive' pilots were unwilling to intervene—even when they had information that might save the plane."[5] This impacted not only the crew's psychological safety but the physical safety of their passengers as well.

As O'Toole and Bennis argue, candor runs both ways— top to bottom and bottom to top. When leaders lack candor, transparency suffers as followers choose to perpetuate the status quo rather than speak the truth. Nobody wants to ruffle the boss's feathers, because they've learned that the boss cares more about knowing everything rather than admitting what you don't know. As a consequence, *everyone* in the organization sacrifices their candor. Information ceases to flow freely, and key details never see the light of day. If we're going to find and cultivate real influence, we need to become those who resist the urge to "put on a show" and, instead, rediscover the power of candor.

Courage: Being Courageous

We turn to courage last, although it is certainly not the least. As Maya Angelou wrote, "Courage is the most important of all the virtues, because without courage you can't practice any other virtue consistently." Before Angelou, Winston Churchill said something similar: "Courage is rightly esteemed the first of human qualities, because, as has been said, it is the quality which guarantees all others."[6] Without the courage to sacrifice our pride for the sake of others, we can never truly be civil. Without the courage to be open and honest with others, we can never become people of candor. Without the courage to exercise our true power, we will always be tempted to keep it under wraps.

In 2014, the newly minted CEO of General Motors, Mary Barra, sat before a hostile committee of senators as they grilled her over a spate of fatal car crashes. The deaths had been linked to a defective ignition switch in the popular Chevrolet Camaro, and Barra was called to give an account for her company's negligence. Rather than deflect responsibility to her predecessors, Barra willingly took the heat herself.

More than that, she personally owned the deep cultural dysfunction that had led to such a disastrous outcome. As of this writing, Barra remains at the helm of GM. Although American carmakers continue to struggle in various ways, she has held on to her influence in both the company and her industry by remaining a woman of great courage.

Whether it's the CEO who refuses to wilt under the pressure of government oversight or the general who personally leads his troops into battle, people instinctively admire courage. In Chapter 4, we'll look more closely at what courage is and what it isn't, but for now we can define it as the strength to act in the face of fear and uncertainty. Courage is often understood as fearlessness, but that's an unfortunate mistake. The key to courage isn't acting like we're not afraid but rather owning our fear and refusing to let it stop us. When our heads tell us to run, courage is the victory of a *heart* that says "Stay."

Executives and military officers notwithstanding, courage doesn't matter only for the leader of an organization. "Ordinary" people are faced every day with opportunities to display extraordinary courage. We saw it with Harold Cottam, who courageously bucked his chain of command to tell his captain that the *Titanic* was in trouble. We also saw it in the cardiac nurse who had the gall to schedule a little girl even though past practice had proven that her mother's complaints were fruitless. The Power of One is the power of courage—the nerve to lean right into the moment with everything we've got.

Conclusion

Think back to the introduction to this chapter. Positionally, Joe and Jane are on the same track. Dispositionally, Joe is miles ahead, and the team he's built around him is poised to go farther and faster than Jane's ever could. That's the power of one person who embodies the virtues of civility, candor, and courage to influence others for the better. That's the power of a junior executive—a "nobody" as far as most organizational charts are concerned—to create real and lasting change in the lives of his immediate coworkers and, through them, the entire organization. It's the Power of One small part that reverberates throughout the whole.

The default mode is crouching at every one of our doors, and its desire is that we would ignore our power and slink back toward lives of feckless impotence. It's time for us to fight back, to embrace the Power of One and cultivate the virtues that will allow us to exercise real influence in the lives of others. Are you ready to become the kind of leader who uses civility, candor, and courage to make a real difference in the world? Then get ready, because this is where the rubber really hits the road.

Notes

1. Jules Norwood, "NO MORE SILENCE: Black Lives Matter Co-founder Calls for Action, Change," *ECU*, February 29, 2016, accessed October 5, 2021 from https://news.ecu.edu/2016/02/29/no-more-silence/.
2. James O'Toole and Warren Bennis, "A Culture of Candor," *Harvard Business Review*, June 2009.
3. Ibid.
4. Ibid.
5. Ibid.
6. Winston Churchill, *Unlucky Alfonso* (New York: Collier and Son, June 27, 1931, Page 49).

Chapter 5

What Is Civility?

In 1898, 3,000 educators attended the First Pedagogical Conference in Turin, Italy.[1] As they gathered, recent events weighed heavy on their hearts. Empress Elizabeth of Austria-Hungary had just been stabbed to death by an Italian anarchist—the third in a string of assassinations carried out by his fellow countrymen. Newspapers across Europe instantly blamed the Bel Paese ("Beautiful Country"), denouncing its people as a bunch of uncivilized barbarians. At the conference in Turin, the gathered Italian educators couldn't help but take the world's denunciation personally. Were *they* responsible? Had *their* teaching created a class of anti-social murderers? To help them consider the problem, the conference invited a young medical doctor named Maria Montessori to speak. Montessori's assessment was stark; Italy was guilty as charged. The problem wasn't what they were doing in the classroom. It was what they *weren't* doing that was responsible for this lack of civility.

According to Montessori, the problem laid squarely in Italy's failure to serve mentally handicapped children. Having spent her early career educating these so-called deficients, she was uniquely positioned to call Italian educators out on

DOI: 10.4324/9781003266556-5

their systemic neglect. *This*, Montessori said, was Italy's problem. If the American novelist and advocate for minority rights, Pearl Buck, was right to say that "the test of a civilization is the way that it cares for its helpless members," then Italy had catastrophically failed that test. And the only way to make things right for the sake of the kids and their country, said Montessori, was to develop a new crop of schools dedicated to caring for these "lost" children.

More than just a matter of doing the right thing, educating handicapped children was a matter of political wisdom. It was to be a program of virtue formation meant to *civilize* Italy by teaching it to value the "least" among its citizens (as they were perceived at that time). Soon, Montessori became a national celebrity. Her tireless efforts led to the establishment of the National League for the Education of Retarded Children. Eventually, the educational philosophy that arose out of her work gave rise to a global movement. More than 100 years later, schools that bear her name exist all over the world, all because of her devotion to this very concrete form of developing national civility. The Power of One.

Civility and the Power of Citizenship

What do you think about when you read the word *civility*? Is it a few politicians having a principled, yet gracious argument? Do you envision a couple of prim and proper women sitting down to a fancy cup of tea? Perhaps, you're thinking of an elderly man holding the door open for his wife. Or maybe it's a divorced husband and wife who manage to ward off their bitterness for the sake of their small children.

Civility encompasses all of those scenarios. As we're about to see, though, civility is about much more than "being nice." You may have noticed that the word itself looks a bit like "civilization." Indeed, the two words are related. The ancient Latin roots of the word (*civis, civitas, civilitas*) revolved around the art and science of being a citizen of a particular civilization. To be civilized quite literally meant to be a productive member of a certain country. Over the course of history, however, *civility* (from the French *civilité*) came to describe the basic features of human behavior and what we all owe one another, not just as citizens of a particular civilization but the entire human race.

Today, *civility* is a word you'll often hear on TV. As our political conversation gets more heated, talking heads from both sides call upon Americans to treat one another with civility. That message isn't exactly controversial. According to a report from Weber Shandwick and Powell Tate, 69% of Americans agree that incivility is a major problem in our society.[2] At one level, the call to civility is simply a charge to *be good humans.* We should all treat one another with decency and respect. However, the call to civility in our public discourse often appeals to more than just our humanity; it seeks to build on our common ground *as Americans.* We're all a part of the same national project, and we all have a vested interest in its success. Our country is an exceptional place where argument isn't discouraged or suppressed; it's welcome, because we know that when many perspectives come together, the result is something far richer than anything any one person could've produced on his or her own.

When it comes to disagreement in policy and politics, the problem isn't so much *that* we disagree as it is *how* we disagree. To be civil in public discourse is to disagree *well*—to recognize that the conversations we have are meant to contribute to the prosperity of our nation and the well-being of *all* its citizens. They're not about slaying your opponents or scoring cheap political points. They're about uncovering a truth that will benefit society as a whole. When Maria Montessori stood before 3,000 fellow educators, her goal wasn't to win an argument or to establish herself as a national celebrity (though, she did both). Instead, her chief aim was to lift marginalized children out of obscurity and civilize a nation in the process. *That's* why the people listened and followed her lead.

Civility is citizenship. It's the power of subordinating our individual wishes and desires for the sake of the greater good. The most civil citizens are the most powerful ones because their genuine desire to build up rather than tear down establishes them as people of positive influence in their neighbors' eyes. This applies at every level—from our citizenship in the United States all the way down to the kind of "citizenship" we enjoy in our homes, neighborhoods, and workplaces. When we're civil with one another, we're not just showing people the dignity and respect they deserve as human beings. We're acknowledging that we're in this together, and we're honoring an unspoken pledge to work together for the good of our families, communities, and organizations. That's a beautiful thing. More importantly for this book, it's a *powerful* thing and a key to developing our ability to influence others.

What Civility Looks Like

So far, we've talked about civility at a high level. But what does it look like on the ground? How do we "spot" civility? In the following two lists, I offer some marks or attributes of civility in others. I've given two lists instead of one because it's important to distinguish between the individual and collective aspects of civility. This first list focuses on the individual— what you can expect to see in a civil *person*. Keep in mind: my lists are neither absolute nor exhaustive. You might encounter an individual who always says please and thank you, yet still treats their neighbors with disrespect. With that caveat in mind, here are seven things you can expect to see in a civil coworker or neighbor:

1. **Respect**—Respect is the engine that drives civil behavior. You may not always be able to quantify or demonstrate how, but the speech, behavior, and mannerisms of a civil person are always marked by respect for others.
2. **P's & Q's**—Civil people generally demonstrate their care and concern for others by using simple phrases such as "please" and "thank you." This isn't absolute, but good manners can speak volumes about whether a person values others.
3. **Ownership**—Civility takes honesty. People who own their failures and apologize for their mistakes show that they care more about the greater good than their own individual success.
4. **Service**—You can't have civility without service. A civil person routinely puts others before him- or herself, actively looking for opportunities to help their fellow citizens succeed.
5. **Positivity**—Civility breeds positivity. The most civil people in a workplace are those who regularly embody a positive attitude, choosing to not allow negativity to overcome the culture.
6. **Empathy**—Truly civil people are able to step into others' shoes and go for a walk. They look beyond their own view of things, put on the perspective of their coworker, and try to experience the world from that person's point of view.
7. **Sympathy**—Civil people don't just seek to understand the other person's perspective; they also display genuine compassion when others are struggling.

Civil people make for civil communities and workplaces. As neighbors and coworkers embody the marks listed previously, we see their civility transform the organizational cultures they inhabit. The following marks are what you can expect to see in a workplace or community that has been "civilized" in this way:

1. **No-Gossip Zone**—Respect for others keeps civil people from engaging in gossip. In a positive environment shaped by civility, gossip comes across as more of a betrayal than a hobby. Civil people won't stand for it.
2. **Zero Tolerance for Misconduct**—Civil workplaces and communities dignify each citizen and refuse to give cover to those who don't. They do this because it's the right thing to do *and* it promotes the health of the organization.
3. **Relational Harmony and Inclusivity**—Civil workplaces refuse cultural conformity and welcome and appreciate differences. They ensure that every employee has a sense of belonging and inclusion and is unafraid to "let their freak flag fly"!
4. **A Safe Space for Disagreement**—Civil people get along, not because they sacrifice their convictions but because they use them as a means to serve. People engage in honest debate so that *together* they can find the best way forward.
5. **Engagement**—In an uncivil environment, people check out and operate in the default mode I described earlier. In a civil workplace or community, they will be proactive and intentional for the sake of the greater good.

Are You Really Civilized?

In the following chapters, we're going to dive more deeply into the nuts and bolts of civility: why it's lacking in corporate America, what the dangers of incivility are, and what we can do about it as individuals and organizations. As we do, we'll drill down into specific ways in which you can cultivate civility in your own life and that of others around you. Before we get there, though, it's important that you pause for a moment and take some time to reflect on your own level of civility. This book is written to help us all on our journey toward personal power and influence. As with any journey, you need to know where you are before you chart a path to your destination.

Would people describe you as a civil person? The best way to find out, of course, is to ask them! But before you start polling your friends and coworkers, take some time to reflect honestly on your own answer to that question. I think most of us would like to consider ourselves civil, but our actions and attitudes may ultimately reveal otherwise. For that reason, we need to be honest and objective in our self-assessment. To that end, I've provided this simple diagnostic.

Reflect on each of the following statements and mark down, on a scale of 0 to 5, whether you disagree or agree. If you always say please and thank you, for example, then mark down a number 5 for statement 1. If you *never* say it, then you'd mark down a 0.

1. I regularly say please and thank you.
2. I don't participate in gossip and shut it down when I hear it.
3. I own my mistakes instead of shifting blame.
4. I go out of my way to help others, dropping what I'm doing to give them aid.
5. I treat others with respect by speaking well of them and with candor.
6. I include coworkers in both work projects and social conversations even if I am uncomfortable with their differences.
7. I focus on positive dialogue with my peers, even when I have critical feedback.
8. I go out of my way to spend time with people outside of my demographic.

Once you're done working through the statements, add up your numbers and check them against the following civility scale:

- 34–40 Fred Rogers: the paragon of civility
- 27–33 Emily Post: mostly civil with the occasional slide
- 20–26 Henry Jekyll: sometimes civil, sometimes monstrous
- 13–19 Archie Bunker: rarely civil, mostly abrasive
- 0–12 Hagar the Horrible: the uncivilized barbarian

Conclusion

How'd you do on the civility assessment? If you found out you're Fred Rogers, then good for you. You're already well on your way to discovering the power and influence that comes from exercising civility in our everyday lives. If you're at the other end of the spectrum, then this isn't the time for despair. Wherever you

Maria Montessori.

Photo: Shutterstock

land on the scale, the following chapters are for you. Although Hagar obviously needs some work, even Mr. Rogers could stand to learn more about civility and how to grow in it. In Chapter 7, that's precisely what we'll consider. Before we get there, though, we need to pause and consider the dangers of incivility, particularly in the workplace. To that we now turn.

Notes

1. Larry Schaefer, "History and Civility," accessed from https://files. eric.ed.gov/fulltext/EJ1078021.pdf.
2. "Civility in America 2018: Civility at Work and in Our Public Squares," *Weber Shandwick and Powell Tate, in partnership with KRC Research,* accessed October 5, 2021 from www. webershandwick.com/wp-content/uploads/2018/06/Civility-in-America-VII-FINAL.pdf.

Chapter 6

Incivility and the Impact of Bad Citizenship

We all know what incivility looks like when we see it—insensitive comments, inconsiderate behavior, downright abrasiveness. But for all the individual annoyance of an uncivil employee, the cultural impact of incivility is the worst. In Chapter 1, I shared the story of Maria Diaz—a woman who fought for years to build a successful career only to lose her life tragically under the pressure of a toxic workplace. More and more stories like hers are coming to the surface in the wake of #MeToo and the racial reckoning. Some of them seem minor—an uncomfortable microaggression or an inappropriate comment. Others are far worse—extended harassment, systemic inequities, outright prejudice, or battery. Big or small, minor or major, all of these stories represent an unacceptable state of affairs in the American workplace writ large.

The Cost of Incivility

Although we always want to be careful about simplistic explanations, I believe incivility lies at the core of our workplace

DOI: 10.4324/9781003266556-6

dysfunction. According to Christine Porath and Christine Pearson—both professors of management and noted researchers on civility—incivility has been on the rise in American corporate culture. This uptick has taken a demonstrable toll on many people. Porath and Pearson surveyed 800 managers across 17 industries to learn what they had to say about employees who'd been the victims of incivility. Here's what they found[1]:

- 48% decreased their work effort.
- 47% spent less time at work.
- 38% decreased the quality of their work.
- 63% lost work time avoiding their uncivil peer(s).
- 66% noticed a decline in their performance.
- 78% noticed a decline in their commitment to the organization.
- 25% admitted to taking their frustration out on customers.
- 12% left their jobs.

According to Porath and Pearson, incivility harms companies not only at the individual level, but at the organizational level as well. Uncivil workplaces are uncreative and unproductive. Team spirit suffers and customers are turned off by a pervasive atmosphere of rudeness—regardless of whether ill treatment is ever targeted at them. "Whether it's waiters berating fellow waiters or store clerks criticizing colleagues," say Porath and Pearson, "disrespectful behavior makes people uncomfortable, and they're quick to walk out without making a purchase."[2] Incivility is ugly, and customers won't stick around to do business with an organization that allows it to fester.

Lost revenue isn't the only bottom-line consequence of incivility. Porath and Pearson also follow Accountemps and Fortune to report that "managers and executives at Fortune 1,000 firms spend 13% of their work time—the equivalent of seven weeks a year—mending employee relationships and otherwise dealing with the aftermath of incivility."[3] As I've learned firsthand, consulting costs and attorney's fees only compound those losses when organizations are forced to seek outside help. The bottom line is this: the cost of incivility is far too high for companies to treat it lightly.

What Makes for a Bad Corporate Citizen?

In the previous chapter, I described civility as something more than being nice to your neighbor. At its core, civility is about good citizenship—recognizing the inherent value others bring to the organization and working together to move forward in a positive direction. If you have that, then you'll have all the trappings of civility—respect, manners, positivity, etc. On the flip side, incivility is another name for bad citizenship. Where you have a handful of self-centered employees who care more about themselves than the team and their colleagues, you can expect to find all the marks of incivility—disrespect, rudeness, negativity, and worse.

Bad citizens come in many shapes and sizes:

■ The abrasive middle manager who can't help belittling her team members.
■ The disengaged assembly worker with a chip on his shoulder.
■ The person who cares more about his numbers than the success of the team.
■ The person who can't stop talking about coworkers behind their backs.

These are the more obvious forms of bad citizenship, but they're not the only ones. Allow me to illustrate another from my own experience. As I shared earlier in the book, I took on my first role in law before I went to law school. As office manager, one of my jobs was to see that the front desk was covered when the receptionist took her breaks. I'd usually assign one of our "runners" to the task—college kids who'd handle odd jobs around the office for a little extra cash. One day, I scheduled a young man named Chase to fill the position. The job was easy, and he had everything he needed. No sweat, right? Wrong. As Chase manned the phones, one of the named partners came rushing into my office. "Why is Chase at the front desk?" he fumed. When I told him that Chase was merely filling in, the partner exploded, "He's a guy! He can't be out there! Our clients want to be greeted by a woman!" Without giving it a second thought, I jumped out of my seat, ran to the desk, kicked Chase out of the chair, and covered the phones until our receptionist returned.

As I sat and reflected on what had just happened, my mind raced. What had I done wrong? Was it really that big a deal if a guy sat at the front desk? Later that day, Chase hunted me down and asked why I'd hurried him out of the chair. When I told him, we both shook our heads and laughed. After that, I never asked another guy to cover for the receptionist again. It wasn't until I took my first employment law class in school that I realized I was probably breaking the law. Worse, I was complicit in our partner's incivility. I didn't have the language for it yet, but he wasn't being a very good citizen—and neither was I.

Biased Citizenship and the Danger of a Single Story

When that partner rushed in and had me kick Chase off the front desk, he made a tactical plunder. He tied me—the salaried office manager—up with reception work when I had other, more pressing matters to attend to. His outmoded view of gender in the office functionally transformed me into just some generic female—an interchangeable automaton to be thrown behind a desk rather than employed in other meaning-ful work. He also shrunk my pool of available candidates to fill the front desk position, hamstringing my ability to orga-nize my labor in the most efficient and effective way possible. Whatever we want to say about the morality of it, his gender bias was just plain bad business.

This kind of thing happens every day. Biased thinking replaces concrete individuals with abstract categories. It leads us to judge people according to their background and appear-ance rather than skill and potential. We then fit them into roles based on whether they look the part vs. whether they can deliver results. We put the wrong people in the wrong places and end up with a team that fails to perform at peak capacity. This is how our little civilizations crumble, and it's all sourced in an original posture of incivility.

As an HR professional, I've evaluated my fair share of can-didates in the workplace. I've seen how discrimination, ageism, racism, and stereotyping have influenced virtually every person-nel decision there is. You'd be amazed at the number of times I've seen an inferior candidate win out based on little more than the sound of his name, the prestige of the school he attended, or the color of her skin. Sometimes, these decisions come from explicit prejudice. Most of the time, though, they're made implicitly—underneath leaders' conscious radar. Whether we are talking about a police officer's unacknowledged tendency to be more suspicious of one particular ethnic group over all others or a hiring manager's subconscious penchant for dismiss-ing applications with names he can't pronounce, implicit bias creates uncivil environments by subtly (or not so subtly) com-municating that only certain types of citizens are valued here.

Implicit bias, Jenée Desmond-Harris explains, "comes to life" in the form of microaggressions.[4] An Asian person who is told they are "articulate"; a physically disabled person who is spoken to like a child although they have multiple college degrees—these are just a few examples of the microaggressive ways in which our implicit biases bubble up to the surface in everyday life. These microaggressions, Desmond-Harris says, "are more than just insults, insensitive comments, or generalized jerky behavior." Rather, these behaviors

> are painful because they have to do with a person's membership in a group that's discriminated against or subject to stereotypes. And a key part of what makes them so disconcerting is that they happen casually, frequently, and often without any harm intended, in everyday life.

Microaggressions create a habitually insensitive workplace in which the everyday behavior of some employees tells others that they are less valued and less welcome in the workplace—whether the microaggressors intend to communicate these sentiments or not. The resulting environment is anything but inclusive, as the subjects of these microaggressions are made to feel small, inferior, and unable to do their best work.

In her powerful TED Talk, "The Danger of a Single Story," Chimamanda Ngozi Adichie sheds light on the kinds of implicit bias that infect our engagement with people unlike ourselves. Speaking at a cultural level, she warns that "if we hear only a single story about another person or country, we risk a critical misunderstanding." We paint entire cultures with a single brush and, in the process, delude ourselves about their true nature. We trade the truth about entire swaths of people for a lie of our own making. We make assumptions about people based on their cultural heritage or skin color, and those assumptions inevitably express themselves in our thoughts, words, and actions. Tragically, we fail to understand people as they really are and, instead, we acquaint ourselves with a caricature based on who we think they should be.

What I've learned during my years as a human resources professional is how much weight the "single story" carries in the minds of so many executives in America. These are the kinds of stories and biases that I've uncovered in my professional journey:

∎ Black women are too aggressive and too ambitious.
∎ Mexicans are migrant workers, domestics, and are here illegally.
∎ Asians are good at math and science.
∎ Black men are intimidating.
∎ Older workers are no good with technology.
∎ Mothers are not committed to their professions.
∎ Disabilities are visible and physical.
∎ White men are educated and successful.

When we allow these stereotypes to shape our thoughts and actions, we engage in bad citizenship. We not only act with incivility toward the people we reject on the basis of our own prejudice, but we also deprive our organizations of the true value these people could bring. We stick the Asian woman in an accounting role when she would really excel in a role that exercised her creativity. We take the mother off a key project on the assumption that she'll be too distracted by her family commitments to see it through. In each case, we use the wrong human tool for the job—frustrating them and sabotaging our team's success. Even worse, our stereotypical thinking leads us to cultivate environments in which every book is judged by its cover and not its contents. We create fundamentally uncivil organizations that struggle to rise above mediocrity and ultimately fall when the lawsuits start rolling in.

To be clear, the assumptions we make about people don't always carry the kind of racial or cultural freight I pointed to above. The categories we use to judge other people often revolve less around "white" and "brown" and more around words such as "educated" and "uneducated," "lazy" and "ambitious," "criminal record" and "clean slate." Although there's a certain logic to these kinds of distinctions, they also perpetuate incivility because they force us to make huge assumptions about other people—assumptions that are often based in anything but fact. I recently took to LinkedIn to share about this, and more than 12 million people from various backgrounds, industries, professions, and levels of influence resonated with what I had to say:

- Breaking News!!!!
- I hired someone that didn't shake my hand firmly during the interview. He rocked as an employee.
- I hired someone with three typos on their resume. She was the most detail-oriented person I've ever worked with.
- I hired someone without a college degree. He was way smarter, more innovative, and creative than me!
- I hired someone with four kids. Never met someone so devoted and committed to her career.
- I hired someone who had been incarcerated as a young adult. He's a VP now.
- I hired someone over 60. She taught me some tricks on Excel that I use to this day!
- Can we please throw out all those silly assumptions and rules that we've made up in our head about what a person needs to be, look like, have accomplished, and do, to succeed?
- In my experience, as an HR leader and as a hiring manager, it's those that typically don't get a "shot" who tend to kick butt in the workplace!
- So, before you throw that resume away because they don't have every certificate and degree—or—don't call back that candidate because they didn't give you a firm handshake—think about trying something new. Someone new.

Whether we've been the employer or the employee, we've all had to learn the "conventional wisdom" about the hiring process. I alluded to much of it above (give a firm handshake, look an interviewer in the eye, dress to impress, proofread your resume, etc.). A great deal of that wisdom is rooted in solid experience and human psychology. However, much of it is crusted over with the conventions and expectations of a bygone era. And the fact of the matter is that too many hiring managers out there rely on tired, outdated tropes to help them weed through barely manageable stacks of applications. But they must realize that, so long as they keep on using these uncivil means to build their workforce, they weave incivility into the very fabric of their companies. On top of that, they deprive themselves of all those people who *could've* kicked butt for them in the workplace.

The First, the Only, and the Power of One

After law school, I chose not to practice law in the courtroom. Instead, I decided to bring my legal expertise to corporate America. Since then, I've enjoyed the distinct privilege of being the "first" and the "only" on more occasions than I can count: the first Black person to reach the C-suite, the only woman in a room full of decision-makers, and so on. For perfectly understandable reasons, many people find situations such as these intimidating. If you're the first, then your gut feeling is to stay quiet. If you're the only, then you better lay low and just be grateful for your seat at the table. Don't get me wrong; I've always been grateful for my seat, but I've also never doubted that I belong there. When you're the first and/or the only one of your kind at the table, it's on you to use your Power of One to speak up and change things for the better. You may be the first, but you won't be the last. You may be the only, but not for long.

Given my experience, you'd think I'd be the last person in the world to let my bias get the best of me. Think again.

While I was in law school at the University of Arkansas, my husband was a teacher. Northwest Arkansas was not a very diverse place. Aside from the basketball coach, my husband was the only person of color on the faculty of more than 100. It was often assumed he was a football coach or the custodian when in fact he taught AP World History. The student population at that time was about 80% white and 20% Hispanic. The Hispanic student population intrigued my husband. Eager to learn more about his students' culture, he participated in a summer program in which he got to travel to Saltillo, Mexico, and stay with a host family.

Once my husband arrived, he called to tell me the family he was staying with included a college professor and an engineer. My mouth immediately dropped! It had not occurred to me that there would be households in Mexico with two very well-educated adults. As he continued to share his experience, we both realized how similar our lives were to theirs. Each day, he explored different parts of the town and soon realized that the people there were far safer, cleaner, and friendlier than we'd allowed ourselves to believe. From that experience, we both learned just how much we'd been taken in by the "single story" mentality. We've traveled the world since then and, every time, we've made it a point to get to know each location on its own terms. Without exception, the many cultures we visited were nothing like what we'd come to expect.

Learning about the citizens and appreciating the diverse cultures of other countries taught me to be a better citizen in my own country. In the office, especially, it forced me to reexamine my own biases and how they impacted my decision-making process. I began to pay closer attention to the ways I assumed what someone would look like when I read their name on their resume. I began to discard my predilection for the Ivy League. More importantly, I became curious. With that curiosity, I was able to suss out and unveil the underrepresentation of others. I began to see that there were other "firsts" and "onlys" that I could bring to the table. Through all that, I was able to prove to myself and others that, by casting aside our bias and prejudice, we give people the opportunity to far exceed our expectations. All it took was a commitment to exercising my power and influence for the good of our organization and its people—civility in its truest sense. As a result, the invisible became visible, the forgotten remembered, and the lost found.

Conclusion

Incivility is about so much more that poor manners and abrasive employees. The stakes around civility are infinitely higher than merely creating a "nice office environment." What we've looked at in this chapter are the insidious ways in which incivility and bad citizenship ruin organizations from the inside out. Whether it's the individual turmoil that results from a discrete act of incivility or it's the culture-level infection that comes from unchecked and pervasive bias, bad citizenship is threatening to destroy the places we call work and home. It's up to us to wield our Power of One to become the best of citizens—to put on civility and inspire others to do the same. We'll see what that looks like in the next chapter.

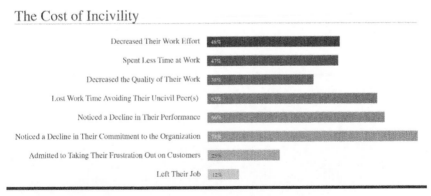

The Cost of Incivility

Decreased Their Work Effort	48%
Spent Less Time at Work	47%
Decreased the Quality of Their Work	38%
Lost Work Time Avoiding Their Uncivil Peer(s)	63%
Noticed a Decline in Their Performance	66%
Noticed a Decline in Their Commitment to the Organization	78%
Admitted to Taking Their Frustration Out on Customers	25%
Left Their Job	12%

The cost of incivility.

Notes

1. Christine Porath and Christine Pearson, "The Price of Incivility,"
Harvard Business Review, January-February, 2013.
2. Ibid.
3. Ibid.
4. Jenée Desmond-Harris, "What Exactly is a Microaggression?"
Vox Magazine, February 15, 2016, accessed October
5, 2021 from www.vox.com/2015/2/16/8031073/
what-are-microaggressions.

Chapter 7

How to Become a Model Citizen

Katherine Johnson (then, Coleman) grew up in West Virginia in the 1920s. As an African-American, her early passion for arithmetic was nearly snuffed out by her local school system's refusal to educate Black children past the eighth grade. When her parents managed to find a high school for her to attend, Katherine immediately excelled. She managed to enroll at West Virginia State University at the age of 14 and graduated *summa cum laude* four years later with degrees in mathematics and French. In 1939, she became one of the first three African-American students to attend graduate school at West Virginia University. After leaving WVU to focus on her family, Katherine taught in segregated schools for more than a decade. In 1952, she went to work for NASA's predecessor, the National Advisory Committee for Aeronautics (NACA). For the next 35 years, Katherine served her country as a master of complex manual calculations. She was instrumental in the *Apollo* and Space Shuttle programs.

Despite her mathematical genius, Katherine faced significant obstacles on account of her race and gender. Her

DOI: 10.4324/9781003266556-7

intelligence was questioned, her presence was met with resistance, and others routinely took credit for her work. Nevertheless, Katherine persisted because she believed in the work NASA was doing. Her knowledge and skill quickly earned her a positive reputation among her male bosses and colleagues. To the extent that she could, Katherine ignored the barriers, asserted herself respectfully, and demanded a seat at every table that would have her. Eventually, those barriers would tumble, and Johnson would come to be known as a trailblazer for African-Americans *and* women in science. In 2015, President Barack Obama proudly draped the Presidential Medal of Freedom over Katherine's 97-year-old shoulders and lauded her as a "pioneer who broke the barriers of race and gender, showing generations of young people that everyone can excel at math and science and reach for the stars."[1]

Looking for Civility in an Uncivil World

From her earliest years, Katherine was the victim of an uncivil society. Her hometown in West Virginia failed to nurture her unique gifts. Her colleagues at NASA refused to acknowledge her distinct contribution. As the 2016 film *Hidden Figures* demonstrates in dramatic detail, Katherine slogged through more sexist and racist sewage than you or I could ever imagine. Even so, she never stopped moving forward with poise and class. She truly *believed* in NASA and what she had to contribute to the world through it. So, she returned good for evil as often as she could and powered through doing the work she knew would benefit their mission—whether anyone noticed or not.

We've come a long way since the segregation of the 1920s and the sexism of the 1950s. Even so, incivility is on the rise in our country, particularly in our workplaces.[2] Approximately 69% of Americans blame the internet, but I think the problem is much more analog than that. There was once a time in which workplace relationships were friendly, yet formal; familiar, but not without a proper sense of distance. As businesses have grown more and more casual, that professional distance between colleagues has all but vanished, leaving a workplace in which the patterns of civil interaction have been replaced by an interpersonal free-for-all.

As the saying goes, familiarity breeds contempt, and the erosion of workplace civility has led to patterns of uncivil interaction that only exacerbate the problem:

- We thank less and demand more.
- We email instead of call.
- We subtweet rather than hash out our differences.
- We don't talk; we shout.
- We don't critique; we criticize.
- We don't encourage; we belittle.
- We lose sight of the intrinsic value our colleagues and coworkers bring to the table and, instead, ask questions such as "what have they done for me lately?"

We lack decorum—that deep sense of what it means to "act right" in the workplace. And because we lack decorum, the patterns listed above serve to create a corporate culture in which civility takes a backseat to utility. Might makes right as we lose all sense of what constitutes normal human decency and, instead, we interact with others based on the cash value they bring to our lives or that of the organization. Instead of recognizing and honoring the inherent dignity of others, we make them earn our respect. And when that respect is based simply in performance, we lend power and prestige to people who are unprepared to wield it for the good of others.

When incivility runs free, we let our rainmakers push the envelope. We look past their abhorrent behavior and straight to their impact on the bottom line. We turn a blind eye to repeated complaints and legitimate grievances, all because we "know" our organization couldn't survive without this key leader or that top salesperson. We ignore our biases, downplay our weaknesses, and let each other off the hook when we should be calling one another to a higher standard of civil behavior in the workplace. And, as a result, we create increasingly toxic workplaces that militate against human flourishing and stamp out creativity. It's high time we stop giving incivility a free pass and strive for *more*. If you and I are serious about cultivating influence, then it's up to *us* to use our Power of One to set a more civil tone. But how will we do that?

Recovering the Virtue of Civility

At the end of the day, our civility problem isn't going to be solved in the C-suite, the human resources department, or the state legislature. It needs to be solved in our hearts first—in the everyday attitude each one of us brings into the workplace. The pervasive incivility that's taken hold in American workplaces isn't just a product of poor leadership; it's a product of a deep loss in each one of us. If we're going to remedy that loss, we need to recover civility as a virtue and actively work to cultivate it in our lives.

Virtue is an old-fashioned word, but it's a crucial one if we're going to learn how to be civil with one another. Rosalind Hursthouse and Glen Pettigrove define virtue as

> an excellent trait of character . . . well entrenched in its possessor—something that, as we say, goes all the way down, unlike a habit such as being a tea-drinker—to notice, expect, value, feel, desire, choose, act, and react in certain characteristic ways.[3]

To possess the virtue of civility, then, is not just to do civil things but to *be* a civil person. Like Katherine Johnson, such a person responds with civility no matter how uncivil his or her circumstances may be.

Understood as a virtue, civility is more like a reflex than a conscious action. Civil people don't stop and think about *how* to be civil. They don't have to say to themselves, "The civil thing to do would be to help Mary with her caseload. I want to be a civil person. Therefore, I will help Mary with her caseload." No, they just get up and help Mary without a second thought as to why they should do it. This kind of behavior pervades the civil person's contribution at work, in the home, and out in the community. It's a thing of beauty—never contrived, always honest, and genuinely geared toward the good of others. As a virtue, civility is palpable; it demands notice, and it commands influence. The question: how will we cultivate that virtue? The answer: it takes practice.

Practicing Virtue: How to Become a Civil Person

If you'll indulge me for a moment, the average major-league fastball travels at around 95 miles per hour.[4] At that speed, batters only have about one-tenth of a second to judge the pitch and decide whether they're going to swing. With such little time to react, it should be impossible to hit a fastball. But, of course, major league batters do it all the time. How? As it turns out, the human brain is amazing at recognizing patterns and "seeing the future" based on what it thinks will come next. When a practiced batter sees the pitcher's arm come down, he automatically draws from a deep well of lived experience to judge the pitch and decide whether to swing— all before the ball even leaves the pitcher's hand. If you asked the batter to explain how that works, he wouldn't know what to tell you. It's just what his body knows to do. And how did his body "learn" to do that? Practice. Lots and lots of practice.

Cultivating the virtue of civility (or any other, for that matter) takes *practice.* It means stepping into the metaphorical batting cage and swinging at every opportunity for civility that crosses the plate. At first, that practice will seem contrived. Unlike the truly civil person, you'll constantly be asking yourself in the moment, "What would a civil person do?" Often, it'll mean going outside of your comfort zone to do things that don't come naturally to you. Good! To seek virtue, we have to be willing to venture into uncomfortable territory. In the best and most noble way we can, we're going to have to fake it until we make it.

Ten Practices for Cultivating Civility

To that end, here are 10 practices to take up as you seek to put on the virtue of civility this week. Read these practices each morning. Post them in a prominent place at your desk and revisit them throughout the day. At the end of each day, take another look at the list and ask yourself how you did. Finally, consider what you'll do to improve the next day. Keep it up until you get these practices into your bones. Over time, you'll find they come naturally—almost like a reflex. When that day comes, you'll know the virtue of civility is beginning to take hold in your mind, heart, and actions.

1. **Show up on time.** Sometimes, the most civil thing you can do is pay your coworkers and employers the respect of showing up when you're expected to.
2. **Think before you speak (or email).** Before you talk or type, ask yourself: will my words slay, or will they *serve?* If it's the former, then hold off until you can devise a more constructive way to use your words.
3. **Watch yourself.** Consider how your actions and behaviors impact others. Seek ways to make your interactions with others more positive.

4. **Lend a hand.** Find concrete ways to serve your coworkers and neighbors, even if it's as simple as bringing in a trashcan or holding an elevator door.

5. **Acknowledge and respect differences.** Operating in a diverse workforce means respecting that not everyone thinks and acts like you. You don't have to agree with everyone's points of view, but civility means showing respect toward the people who hold them.

6. **Own your mistakes.** Resist the urge to pass the buck. Next time you mess up, own it. Acknowledge what you did wrong and let others see you work to correct it.

7. **Ask for feedback.** For the most part, we're pretty bad at self-awareness. Seek opportunities to ask people how you're being perceived in general (tone, style, respectfulness, attitude, etc.). Even better, ask them how you came off after a particular encounter.

8. **Praise others.** Seek opportunities to verbally praise others for their work. Don't just offer a trite "Good job!" Instead, make your praise as substantive as you can.

9. **Engage your workplace.** Reach out to others. Be a positive force for engagement as you seek to encourage and inspire your coworkers.

10. **Call out incivility in yourself and others.** Don't allow yourself or others to mistreat their coworkers or neighbors, whether it's through explicitly uncivil behavior of the implicit effects of biased thinking and decision-making. Confront incivility whenever you see it with both truth and grace.

Conclusion

I can imagine what Katherine Johnson went through in the middle of the 20th century; I've seen traces of it in my own experience as an African-American woman. And in those uncivil environments, the last thing I wanted to do was respond with civility. To offer just one of many examples, I used to labor for hours and hours with a flat iron and a can of oil sheen to make my naturally curly hair look like that of my colleagues. The *one time* I chose to wear my natural curls, my boss took one look at me and said, "Wow, your hair is big today! You must not have any important meetings!" Wow, indeed. It took me several more years with the flat iron to get over what, to this person, seemed like a harmless remark. It's only when I learned what discrimination against hair looked like and how it was so prevalent that I was able to embrace my curls in all their glory.

Despite legal remedies such as the CROWN Act (which bans discrimination based on natural hair), too many of us are plagued by incivility in the workplace—big and small. This goes to show that the cure for what ails us won't stem from new legislation (as important as such laws may be) but from a revolution within our hearts and minds. With pervasive incivility all around us, this may seem like a lost cause. You can't let that negativity drag you down. Instead, make the decision to reclaim your Power of One, put on civility, and become a person of influence. In her own way, that's what Katherine did. There's no reason you can't, too.

Portrait of Katherine Johnson.

Credit: NASA

Notes

1. "NASA Facility Honors African American Woman Who Plotted Key Space Missions," *The Guardian*, September 22, 2017, accessed October 5, 2021 from www.theguardian.com/science/

2017/sep/22/hidden-figures-mathematician-katherine-johnson-nasa-facility-open.

2. "Civility in America VII: The State of Civility," *Weber Shandwick and Powell Tate, in partnership with KRC Research,* accessed October 5, 2021 from www.webershandwick.com/uploads/news/files/Civility_in_America_the_State_of_Civility.pdf.

3. Stanford Encyclopedia of Philosophy, "Virtue Ethics," first published July 18, 2003, and revised December 8, 2016, accessed October 5, 2021 from https://plato.stanford.edu/entries/ethics-virtue/.

4. Alex Kuzoian, "Hitting a Major League Fastball Should Be Physically Impossible," *Insider,* April 15, 2016, accessed October 5, 2021 from www.businessinsider.com/science-major-league-fastball-brain-reaction-time-2016-4.

Chapter 8

Creating a Culture of Civility

As incivility heats up in our culture, companies such as Google and Microsoft have adopted a more proactive stance toward safeguarding and cultivating civility in the workplace. Google's new internal community guidelines—put in place after controversy over internal discussions in 2018— were designed to create a respectful conversation on internal discussion boards and in the workplace. Microsoft's Digital Civility Index takes a broader view of culture, inviting leaders from all over the globe to take the Digital Civility Challenge, a fourfold commitment to (1) live the golden rule; (2) respect differences; (3) pause before replying; and (4) stand up for myself and others.[1] These are both worthy efforts to affect cultural change at the "local" and "global" levels.

In the previous chapter, we learned about what it takes to become a civil person. In this chapter, we're going to look at what it takes to cultivate a civil culture—whether that's in the home, out in the neighborhood, or at the office. We saw something like that in Chapter 5, where we learned of Maria

DOI: 10.4324/9781003266556-8

Montessori's efforts to civilize Italy through the education of mentally handicapped children. Here, however, we're going to keep things more local. We're not fixing America; we're fixing our street corners and workplaces across the globe. Paradoxically enough, if we fix enough of our little places, we'll end up fixing America and the world.

Defining Civility and Pursuing It Together

Throughout this section, I've stated repeatedly that civility is about more than being polite. It's about recognizing others' humanity and banding together for the sake of our common interest—whether that's our workgroup or our neighborhood association. So, as much as we need to cultivate the virtue of civility as individuals, civility is a communal project. It's something we have to do together. Remember Doris Miller; this is *our* ship, and unless we each act with extraordinary virtue, it won't survive the onslaught of incivility that threatens to sink it.

At a minimum, this means working together to identify and describe the expectations of a civil environment. Without clear standards, one man's awkward joke is another woman's harassment. One manager's tough love is a junior employee's abuse. The key to workplace civility isn't bickering over who's right and who's wrong but coming together to understand and define which types of behavior are acceptable and which are not. The keyword here is *buy-in*. The process is inviting everyone to the table, and the outcome should be a working definition of civility for your own sphere of activity. There should be both positive and negative aspects to your definition, behavior to be *embraced* as well as behavior to be *rejected*.

Here are just a few examples:

Table   Embracing Civility

Embrace	Reject
Diversity	Prejudice
Flourishing	Workaholism
Encouragement	Harassment
Peace	Collegial Warfare
Respect	Disparagement
Service	Self-Seeking
Accountability	Blame-Shifting
Trust	Micromanagement

When coming together to define civility in the workplace, it's important that leaders think clearly and carefully about their role in creating a civil environment. To do so, they must not only buy into the definition but consider the part they'll play in seeing that it's realized in the workplace. At a minimum, this includes designing and implementing a scheme of specific rewards and recognition for civil behavior as well as accountability for those who act in uncivil ways.

More than carrots and sticks, however, leaders need to embody civility themselves, asking whether they lead by intimidation, hostility, and fear, or by kindness, fairness, and humanity. We'll often find that our employees are conditioned to expect us to lead from a place of incivility. Years ago, a relatively new employee texted me one morning to say she had a flat tire and would be late to work. She even sent a photo of the tire! When she arrived, later on, I sat her down and let her know that she never had to send me "proof" like that again. Unless she gave me a reason not to trust her, her word was all I needed. That kind of civility was foreign to her; she was used to having to justify her actions before managers who assumed the worst of her. My "civil" approach—embodied not just in that level of trust but in flexible work hours, PTO, and a high level of autonomy—created a culture in which she eventually learned to stop trying to justify her existence and start operating as the top performer I already knew her to be.

Exercise: Draft Your Civil Constitution

Whether you're a leader or not, set aside a few hours to sit down and craft your vision of a civil workplace or community group. When you're done, circulate it among trusted colleagues for feedback. Edit, revise, and polish. If you're in a position of authority, adopt this as a working charter for your sphere of influence. If you're not, approach your superiors about adopting the document. If they're not on board, gather a small group of coworkers or fellow volunteers and commit to your constitution together.

Here is a brief example of what your constitution might look like:

"We, the people of accounts receivable, in order to create a more civil work environment, declare the following:

■ We will embrace the diverse gifts each one of our team members has to offer and reject any and all prejudice against them.
■ We will encourage one another to be our best selves at work and will refuse to tolerate anyone who tears others down by way of harassment.
■ We will respect one another's value to the team by offering constructive feedback and criticism and never disparaging others.
■ We will seek to serve the interests of the team before our own.

- We will hold ourselves accountable for mistakes instead of blame-shifting.
- We will trust our teammates to play their part, avoiding micro-management and toe-stepping at all costs.
- We will continually work together to make our work-place a civil environment in which everyone is valued, encouraged, and protected."

Set aside regular meetings to discuss whether and how you've managed to abide by this constitution. How you hold one another accountable is ultimately up to you, and it depends largely on your level of authority and buy-in from the cor-porate brass. Negatively, you could devise a disciplinary sys-tem that penalizes employees for violating the constitution. Positively, you could employ rewards and incentives for those who go above and beyond. In practice, some combination of the two will be ideal.

The Promise of a Civil Culture at Work and in the Community

In the aftermath of 9/11, Americans were in shock that the United States was attacked on its own soil, killing thousands of innocents and unsuspecting people. We watched as first responders from across the country rushed to the scenes looking for survivors, looking for answers, looking for hope. In the days that followed, people across the country felt help-less, yet resolved to do something that would show that we were a unified country that would reject terrorism and acts of violence.

To achieve this, we couldn't rush to the scenes like our first responders or stand on the front lines of some military action. But what we could do and what we did was embrace civility. Although we may not have known anyone who was personally impacted by 9/11, we regarded each other as if we did. We as a nation were hurting, and we responded with empathy, respect, and civility. We treated each other every day as if it could be our last day seeing that person. After listening to sobbing organizational leaders who had lost many, if not all, of their employees to this tragedy, other organizational leaders looked at their workforce in a different light. What the aftermath of 9/11 delivered to us was the promise of civility.

With time, many of us have forgotten what it looked and felt like to embrace cultures of civility. Reflecting on her personal experience and her laboratory work, researcher Christin Porath has laid out several of the personal effects of pervasive incivility: decreased performance, personal stress, cognitive impairment, short-term memory loss, immune deficiency, familial stress, and more.[2] Because individuals' resilience in the face of incivility is genetically hard-wired, "the most effective way to reduce the costs of incivility in the workplace is to build a culture that rejects it."[3] As she goes on to observe, however, very few organizations can actually create and sustain a civil culture. Therefore, her proposed solution is to focus on cognitive and affective thriving. "If you're thriving," Porath says, "you're less likely to worry about a hit or take it as a personal affront, more immune to the waves of emotion that follow, and more focused on navigating toward your goal."[4]

In other words, training up individual mental resilience is the key to dealing with incivility in the workplace. That's true enough; the effect of my chapter on becoming a model citizen isn't just to become a civil person, but to develop a certain resilience in the face of incivility. Even so, we can't be too quick to write off the cultural fix. People make the places in which they work. At the same time, their places make them. If we want to become more civil people, we need to actively seek civility in the workplace. And, if we want to create civil work environments, we need to become more civil people. Of course, this is circular. But the circle is virtuous—not vicious. We can jump on at any point. The question is: will we?

Conclusion: A Plea for Civility

What would it look like if this week, you and I walked into the office and, instead of asking ourselves, "How can I get ahead today?" we asked, "How can I help my team get ahead?" What if, instead of seeing our coworkers as the enemy, we saw them as co-collaborators in a corporate mission that transcends any single one of us? What would change if we refused to belittle our colleagues or if we walked down the hall instead of firing off an angry email or if we truly treated our coworkers the way we'd like to be treated? If our office environment was marked by this kind of this civility—this radical vision of a workplace truly committed to the humanity and welfare of every employee—what sort of fruit might grow out of that soil?

Notes

1. "Promoting Digital Civility," *Microsoft Online Safety*, accessed from www.microsoft.com/en-us/digital-skills/digital-civility?activetab=dci_reports%3aprimaryr6#coreui-areaheading-ywbymfs.
2. Christine Porath, "An Antidote to Incivility," *Harvard Business Review*, April 2016.
3. Ibid.
4. Ibid.

Chapter 9

What Is Candor?

Kim Scott is a well-known expert in Silicon Valley. A former employee at both Google and Apple, Scott now works
as a high-profile CEO advisor, helping top executives from
companies such as Dropbox and Twitter reach their potential. In 2015, Scott stood before a room of top executives
and told them a story from her days at Google. After deliver-
ing what she thought was a stellar presentation, Scott's boss,
Sheryl Sandberg, took her for a walk. As they ambled along,
Sandberg offered a bit of gentle criticism: "You said 'um' a lot."
Scott didn't seem to take her input too seriously. As the conversation progressed, Sandberg gently pressed the point until
Scott finally broke: "You know, Kim, I can tell I'm not really
getting through to you. I'm going to have to be clearer here.
When you say 'um' every third word, it makes you sound
stupid." Message received. Google hired a speaking coach, and
Scott ditched her 'um' problem.[1]

Scott is now the co-founder of Candor, Inc., and her book
Radical Candor has inspired a renaissance of "straight-talk" in
companies. As the incident at Google illustrates, there's a sense
in which an overemphasis on politeness and protection can
obscure the truth and keep employees from hearing the feedback

DOI: 10.4324/9781003266556-9

they need in order to grow. Not everyone, however, is excited about candor. After all, the previous section of this book put a high premium on *civility*—a virtue that drives us to treat others with decency and respect. Doesn't radical candor encourage us to throw civility out the window so that we could offer the pure, unvarnished truth all the time? Yes and no. As we'll see, candor and civility *can* live together. Before we see how, though, we need to take a closer look at just what it means to be candid.

What Is Candor?

In Chapter 4, I defined candor as the integrity of a person's speech, thoughts, and actions. The word comes from the Latin word *candere*, which means "to shine" or "be white" in the sense of brightness or radiance. We get it from the same place we get the English word *candle*. This gives us an apt metaphor for candor—the idea of pure, white light, unfiltered and undiminished by anything external to itself. Candid people shine "their truth" out for all the world to see—whether it's *the* truth or not. They are first and foremost true to themselves, regardless of whether others agree with or appreciate what they have to say.

In the process of being true to themselves, candid people realize what Ursula Burns—one of the very few Black females to reach the level of CEO in a Fortune 500 company—realized, "I was more convincing to myself and to the people who were listening when I actually said what I thought, versus what I thought people wanted to hear me say."[2] When Burns hid her light for fear of rubbing others the wrong way, she became a dull, dimmed-down version of herself. When she learned to let her light shine, she became a far more interesting and compelling person to be around.

All this means that a candid person is a transparent person. They say what they mean, mean what they say, and act in a manner that lines up with their expressed attitudes and beliefs.

There's a sense of *safety* in candor—not in the sense that candid people will never ruffle your feathers (they will), but in the sense that you never have to wonder what they really think or what angle they're trying to play. A candid person may be (but by no means *has* to be) rude, brash, and uncivil, but their intentions are generally transparent:

- A cantankerous boss might rip into your job performance because they're hyper-aware of your contribution (or lack thereof) to the bottom line.
- A straight-to-the-point mentor might read over a draft of your proposal and immediately share with you the 73 reasons why it belongs in the trash because she wants you to put your best foot forward.
- A colleague might not hesitate to tell you your latest presentation was a real bomb, not because she wants to revel in your failure but because she wants to see you do better.

These are instances of candor in which the "straight shooter" genuinely has you or your organization's best interests in mind. For all their lack of tact, you can appreciate the intent behind their sharp feedback. Their candor, as poorly delivered and hurtful as it may be, ultimately comes as a gift. They've shined a light you desperately need to see. Without that light, you'd keep on stumbling in the dark and making a fool of yourself like Kim Scott in the opening to this chapter.

The Case for Candor

If you were in the doctor's office, which of these character traits would you prefer: candor or politeness? That's a false dichotomy, to be sure, but if you had to choose just one, there's no question you'd go for the former. Why? Because the most important thing a doctor can do is *tell the truth* about your condition. It would be evil in the extreme if a doctor withheld crucial information just to protect your feelings. In the same way, we desperately need candor at home and at work. At home, we don't want our spouses to bury their concerns and end up succumbing to resentment. We don't want our kids to navigate their personal challenges alone because they're too afraid we'll judge them for opening up to us. At work, we don't want to guess what our bosses are thinking or what they're expecting. We don't want to wonder what our colleagues *really* think or say about us when we're not around. And we certainly don't want our subordinates to hide things from us. Wherever we are, we want the truth!

We'll get into the potential negatives of letting your unfiltered light shine in a moment. For now, here are five distinct advantages to candor in our interpersonal relationships:

1. **Truth**—Candid people are unwilling to let the truth get buried underneath a heap of niceties and political correctness.
2. **Clarity**—Without candor, messages get obscured by excessive care to word things in the least objectionable way. To draw on Brené Brown, the kindness of clarity is overshadowed by the unkindness of unclarity. The former brings people together; the latter tears them apart.[3]
3. **Correction**—Transparent feedback helps people understand precisely what it is about their behavior or performance that needs to change.
4. **Performance**—Clarity in the system helps leaders quickly diagnose problems and tune the organizational machine for optimal performance.
5. **Accountability**—Candor facilitates the flow of "real talk" between people, allowing them to hold one another accountable without having to worry about whether others will be offended.

These significant advantages have the potential to transform a workplace, home, or neighborhood in dramatic ways. Even so, we have to acknowledge that there is real danger in carelessly obliterating your filter in the name of candor. As much as we want people to "give it to us straight," poorly delivered straight talk can do more harm than good. Here are five ways in which unrestrained candor can cause significant trouble for individuals and organizations alike:

1. **Insensitivity**—There's more than one way to "speak truth," and even if a person's words are all correct, their delivery may be ill-suited to the recipient. This is how people get hurt and teams get torn apart.
2. **Harassment**—There's a difference between communicating the brutal truth and doing it in a brutal way. Candid words delivered in a spirit of anger can be perceived as harassment, especially if they're repeated over multiple occasions.
3. **Misunderstanding**—Candid people shoot straight, but that doesn't mean their aim is always true. When they sound off on matters they haven't quite grasped, they perpetuate misunderstanding and cause relational trouble for no reason.
4. **Too much pressure**—Delivered poorly, candid talk can lay a heavy burden on employees. Candid leaders may not see the wisdom in dialing back the "amount" of truth they deliver. As a result, they crush their hearers under its weight.
5. **Withdrawal**—Some employees shut down in the face of straight talk. Rather than respond constructively, they shrink within themselves.

There is much to be said for candor, but are the potential consequences of unchecked transparency and truth-telling worth the risk? Should we not all agree to "dial it back" in order to protect the safety of our work environment? Perhaps, but I think questions such as these betray an "either-or" approach that ultimately hurts more than it helps. In fact, I believe we can have our candid cake *and* eat it without triggering a lawsuit. Let's find out how.

The Tension: Civility or Candor?

In *Radical Candor*, Scott offers her view on candor as an alternative to three other leadership styles: (1) ruinous empathy, (2) manipulative insincerity, and (3) obnoxious aggression. Style 1 cares too much about people and not enough about challenging them directly. It prioritizes peace over progress and sacrifices growth at the altar of people-pleasing. Style 2 doesn't give a rip about people *or* accountability. It consistently seeks its own ends at the expense of others. Style 3 puts too much emphasis on challenging people and not enough on encouraging them to grow. It tears down, but it doesn't build up.

Radical Candor, Scott argues, strikes the perfect balance between caring and challenging. Radically candid leaders speak the unvarnished truth, but they do so for the good and growth of the *other*—not their own. They're committed to more than simply venting their spleen or tearing others down for sport; they want to see real improvement in the individual and the organization. That's far more important to them than protecting theirs or anyone else's feelings.

Still, that leaves us with a perceived tension between civility and candor. How do we tell the unvarnished truth without creating a hostile work environment? How can we be kind *and* critical? Is that even possible? The tension, I think, arises when we see civility as *merely* about being nice and polite—something akin to ruinous empathy. Scott describes it like this: "When bosses are too invested in everyone getting along, they also fail to encourage the people on their team to criticize one another for fear of sowing discord."[4] In other words, they try to create and organizational unity that exists for its own sake and not for the sake of the mission.

When this happens, employees focus more on keeping the peace than on pursuing meaningful change. The comfortable status quo becomes all-important, and candor represents a mortal enemy to organizational peace and unity. The problem, of course, is that this creates "the kind of work environment where being 'nice' is prioritized at the expense of critiquing and therefore improving actual performance."[5] Nice leaders put the cultural cart before the missional horse. They forget that we're all here to accomplish something—not just to get along and have a good time. In the name of civility, they ironically put their little civilization at risk.

As we learned in Chapter 2 of this book, civility is about *more* than simply being "nice." It's about treating one another with decency and respect *so that* we can work together for the good of the organization. There's nothing in civility that excludes the offering of direct honest feedback. To treat civility as a reason to sugarcoat your coworker's failings is to miss the broader picture and to sacrifice performance at the altar of politeness. That would be a remarkably *un*civil act, for it would deny our fellow citizen the resources and perspective they need to maximize their potential.

Civility encourages thoughtful feedback and pointed encouragement, but it does so with the provision that we treat the other person like a human being and a valued member of the team. Let your criticism *build* others up—not tear them down. It's only through that direct, yet respectful encounter that we can urge one another on toward a more productive vision of citizenship in our organizations.

What we need, then, is both civility *and* candor. In her Ph.D. dissertation, psychologist Keri C. Nelson discovered as much, "finding that employees belonging to profiles characterized by high levels of [safety, civility, and candor] had the most positive work experiences."[6] The key word there is *safety*. Candid people who haven't yet learned the virtue of civility may communicate the truth, but that truth becomes an instrument of psychological harm. On the flip side, civil people who haven't learned the virtue of candor speak kind words but effectively deceive the people they address. Ironically, by allowing them to continue down the wrong path, they inflict their own sort of harm. Imagine the civil coworker who enables her colleague's alcoholism or the team leader who fails to correct a direct report's failure *before* it attracts notice from senior management. In the moment, the decision to withhold the truth for the sake of relational harmony may seem like the safest way to keep the peace and protect the other. In the end, though, it deprives people of the transformative encounter they need in order to move toward true safety.

I know much of this from personal experience. Back while I was working for a large healthcare system, I shared the Director of Human Resources role with another colleague. Let's call her Kate. She was smart and ambitious, and she had her eye set on the same role as I did—Vice President of Human Resources. We both thrived in that competitive environment, which made for a highly productive team. There was just one problem: many of Kate's subordinates did not appreciate her leadership style. They said she was brash and not at all easy to deal with. And when they reported this to our boss, she couldn't bring herself to share it with Kate and, thus, provide her the opportunity to improve the situation. When Kate's subordinates started coming to me instead of her, our healthy competition turned to resentment. She thought I was trying to steal her team away from her. I began to resent both her and my boss on account of all the additional work I had falling into my lap. Eventually, Kate put in her notice. A few short weeks later, I did the same.

What happened here? Whatever else we want to say about this scenario, it seems obvious to me that a lack of candor was to blame. My colleague was a reasonable person who would've gladly received feedback and adjusted her leadership style to better serve her subordinates, but she was never given that chance. My boss's lack of candor deprived her of an opportunity to grow and left her to draw the wrong inference about me and my intentions when she saw employees floating my way. My own lack of candor, as well, contributed to this unfortunate scenario. Had I shared what I was hearing with Kate, we could've thrived together. That's what the Power of One *would* have looked like in this circumstance, and it would've saved this organization from losing two capable senior-level employees within the space of a month.

Conclusion

When Sandberg chose to "get real" with Scott, she opened up an opportunity for true influence. It was only when she dropped the truth-bomb ("you sound stupid") that Scott stopped, listened, and learned. Imagine if Sandberg had let her desire to be nice trump her desire to see Scott grow as an individual. Not only would she have abdicated her Power of One, but she never would've given Scott the nudge she needed to develop her own. Both women's lives would've been poorer for it, and the company they both served would've been that much less effective.

To truly influence others, we need to become people of candor. We have truth to speak to others—truth that is functionally useless until it leaves our lips and enters their ears. To give up that responsibility in the name of civility is to completely misunderstand what civility is all about. Worse, it inflicts real harm when we "see something" but neglect to "say something." In due course, we'll explore how to cultivate the virtue of candor in our lives. Before we do, though, we need to understand how harmful it truly is when we allow ourselves and others to trade candor for darkness. To that, we now turn.

Notes

1. Kim Scott, "Radical Candor—The Surprising Secret to Being a Good Boss," *First Round Review*, accessed from https://firstround.com/review/radical-candor-the-surprising-secret-to-being-a-good-boss/.
2. Ursula Burns, *Brainy Quotes*, accessed from www.brainyquote.com/quotes/ursula_burns_589892.
3. Brené Brown, *Dare to Lead: Brave Work. Tough Conversations. Whole Hearts* (Random House First Addition, New York, October 9, 2018, page 48).
4. Kim Scott, *Radical Candor: Be a Kick-Ass Boss Without Losing Your Humanity* (St. Martin's Press; 1st edition, New York, October 1, 2019, page 32).
5. Ibid.
6. Kerri C. Nelson, "Are Civility and Candor Compatible? Examining the Tension Between Respectful and Honest Work Communication," April 29, 2019, accessed from https://open-commons.uconn.edu/dissertations/2103/.

Chapter 10

Nothing Good Grows in the Dark

In August 2018, the world was shocked to learn of the systemic abuse that had been perpetrated by members of the Roman Catholic clergy in Pennsylvania. Over the course of 70 years, a grand jury discovered, more than 1,000 children had been sexually abused. How was this rampant abuse allowed to carry on in the dark for so many years? In its 900-page report, the grand jury pointed their collective finger starkly in the direction of Church leadership: "the men of God who were responsible for [little boys and girls] did nothing; they hid it all. For decades."[1] The report is hard to read—not so much because of its length but for the depth of its subjects' rank wickedness.

How do six dioceses of the Roman Catholic Church—an organization dedicated to spreading light in the world—end up shrouded in such unspeakable darkness? The answer to that question is far more complex than anything I could offer here. At the root of it all, though, is a complete and utter lack of transparency at virtually every level of the organization. Instead of notifying the authorities and

DOI: 10.4324/9781003266556-10

bringing these egregious acts of abuse out into the light of day, leaders chose to protect their own. In one word, they lacked *candor.* As a result, the cancer of pedophilia was allowed to spread unchecked through the "body of Christ" in Pennsylvania.

Out of the Church and into the Corporate World

It may seem like a far stretch to connect the Roman Catholic Church's troubles with sexual abuse to the corporate world. Sadly, it's not. I've spent enough time around human resources departments to know precisely what a systemic lack of candor can do to perpetuate every kind of workplace misconduct—sexual or otherwise. As a recent high-profile case involving TV personality Bill O'Reilly demonstrates, organizational "untouchables" regularly get away with paying accusers exorbitant amounts of money in exchange for their silence. In less "charitable" circumstances, such as those of Maria Diaz (see Chapter 1), the accuser loses everything while the accused gets off scot free.

It's easy to see how specific cases of abuse and cover-up such as the ones I mentioned earlier might hurt an organization and its people, but there are much more subtle ways in which a lack of transparency or accountability can do harm. Indeed, a pervasive lack of candor is negatively affecting organizations across corporate America. When James O'Toole and Warren Bennis polled 154 executives on the level of transparency in their organizations, "63% of them described their own company culture as opaque."[2] This organizational opacity represents a fairly typical perception, if not always among executives, then certainly among employees who fall lower on the totem pole. They feel like they don't know the "real" story but are simply being fed the company line. Worse, they retreat into their imaginations to discern what's really going on and end up mired in conspiratorial thinking.

In organizations that lack candor, the free flow of information is discouraged, and employees are kept in the dark. Without candor from their leadership, employees can find themselves alienated and adrift. Worse, they are either implicitly or explicitly denied the freedom to tell the truth themselves, leading to an even more pervasive lack of transparency throughout the organization. That systemic lack of candor manifests in a number of ways:

- **Closed Feedback Loops**—Without candor, information doesn't flow freely throughout the organization. Absent clear feedback, underperforming products and processes don't get the attention they need until something breaks.
- **Infrequent or Meaningless Performance Reviews**—Managers treat performance reviews as a formality, as they are often uncomfortable giving candid feedback discussions.
- **No Accountability**—Employees are allowed to underperform or misbehave with impunity. Because no one is willing to call them out, these employees weigh down the team and contribute to employee disengagement.
- **Diminished Performance**—Without a clear mandate and an open flow of performance expectations, employees lack the basic knowledge of what success looks like in their role. As a result, many employees never excel in their careers.
- **Stifled Creativity**—Candor tears down walls; opacity builds them back up. For true collaboration to occur, people need to communicate freely and openly with one another. Without candor, that can't happen.
- **Groupthink**—In organizations where candor is tacitly discouraged, leaders encourage employees to "go along to get along." Instead of inspiring a class of creative collaborators, they groom a troop of yes-people.

■ **Office Politicking**—When everybody has to guess what everybody else is thinking, the result is a hodgepodge of strategic alliances and partnerships that threaten to undermine the cohesiveness of the entire organization.

■ **Psychological Danger**—Employees feel unable to take interpersonal risks such as seeking feedback, asking for help, or admitting a lack of knowledge. As a result, their growth ends up stunted and performance suffers overall.

Darkened and Darkening Habits

The sad truth about darkened organizations is that they've developed so many habits and patterns of secrecy that the deep cultural rut into which they've worked themselves can't help but perpetuate a habitual lack of candor in their employees. Toxic bosses create cultures of silence as fear keeps employees from speaking up, and that lack of feedback encourages further toxicity. Overly sensitive middle managers, for fear of litigation, withhold necessary critique. Their lack of candor only allows bad actors to continue their behavior with impunity. And, in such a dark place, the light is simply not welcome.

It's exceedingly difficult to become a candid person in an organization that discourages candor. If the price we pay for "real talk" is our job, then candor seems very much like a luxury few of us can afford. But is that true? I would argue that we can't afford *not to* get real. The self-harm we inflict when we turn our backs on candor transcends whatever momentary peace we might create at work. Worse, it breeds deep-seated resentment both within us and those around us who desperately need us to stand up and speak the truth they are either unwilling or unable to speak for themselves.

If candor involves a "shining forth" of the truth as we see it, then to lack it is to hide our light under the proverbial bushel. Not only does that promote dishonesty, but it trains us to become people who habitually fudge the truth—often under the self-justifying notion that we're "just being polite" or "keeping the peace." Whatever our reasons—noble (politeness) or ignoble (avoiding a lawsuit), other-serving (protecting feelings) or self-serving (keeping our jobs), the consequence is a further darkening of our own communication patterns and those of the organizations we inhabit.

The following four phenomena represent the darkened habits or patterns of communication that tend to assert themselves in organizational cultures where candor is absent.

Candy-Coated Feedback

We've all had managers who just can't bring themselves to be the bearers of bad news. For example, recall the reluctant boss I mentioned in the previous chapter. She just couldn't bring herself to give my coworker (Kate) the candid feedback she needed in order to be successful. Avoiding uncomfortable words may save a leader from the awkwardness of a tense exchange, but it ultimately only makes matters worse. When the levy of kind words breaks, a flood of overlooked inadequacies will follow as the leader struggles to deal with the fallout of a likely massive failure that otherwise could've been avoided.

Fungal Growth

When it comes to engagement, transparency is essential. When organizations keep employees "in the dark" and fail to maintain a constant flow of transparent communication, they begin to see a "fungal growth" of rumors, gossip, and innuendos. That's not exactly an ideal way to transpire information. The only kind of "growth" you can expect from keeping people in the dark is more akin to black mold than to personal excellence. In an organization without candor, you might be able to raise up an army of dutiful mushrooms who get their work done, but you'll never arrive at the sustainable engagement that takes organizations from good to great.

The Untouchables

As we saw with Harvey Weinstein, Bill O'Reilly, and other faces of the "me too" movement, some organizations tend to be blinded to the misbehavior of "untouchable" employees. These untouchable employees exhibit larger-than-life personas that allowed them to blur the lines between exceptional performance and bad behavior. We've seen and heard of too many of these examples, including gross self-dealing, corruption, and theft—all because the company has been blinded by his larger-than-life persona. Here, I could only multiply examples from my own experience of top performers and indispensable executives who, by virtue of their perceived contribution to the organization, were allowed to get away with all kinds of misconduct.

Litigation "At Will"

False kindness with respect to performance feedback often becomes a serious issue when employees are terminated. Companies who employ their people "at will" can fire them for any reason, so long as it's a *legal* reason. If a jaded employee can make the case that his or her termination was based on illegal grounds (discrimination, retaliation, etc.), then it may fall to the employer to defend themselves in court. If the only performance feedback they have on record for that employee is chock-full of false kindness, then the company will have an exceedingly difficult time proving that they fired the employee on account of anything *other* than the illegal reasons mentioned.

This last point deserves a bit more unpacking, as I've found the least candid companies are the ones who struggle most with letting people go in a way that honors workers, protects teams, and mitigates liability. In my two decades of human resources work, I've often helped leaders determine when and how to terminate employees. Most of the time, these leaders struggled to act, even when it was obvious the employee wasn't a good fit. I was never so hesitant. Why? Because of radical candor. In open and ongoing dialogue, I helped employees discover their challenges and urged managers to address them. When they continued to struggle, I looked for ways to transition them within the company so that they could flourish. We did everything we could so that, if and when termination came, both sides welcomed it as the next logical step rather than an arbitrary decision from on high. This didn't just save face for the employee and litigation costs for the employer. It wielded candor in the most civil way possible—to promote the flourishing of both the individual and the team.

Conclusion

Nothing good grows in the dark. At best, organizations that lack candor discourage the flow of information and hamper their mushrooms' ability to perform at their best. At worst, they create the conditions for misconduct and abuse to spread unchecked throughout the organization. In either case, what's needed most is a rediscovery of candor at both the individual and organizational levels. We need to hear and speak the truth without fear of retaliation. We need to be free to walk in the light.

If the organizations I described here sound familiar to you, and the habits I shared portray behavior you've either experienced or taken part in yourself, then it can be difficult to imagine a path forward. How do we shine the light of candor when we're consumed by the darkness of insincerity and obfuscation? How do we offer *real* talk when everyone around us is content to live in a *virtual* reality? How do we live in a place where candor has been traded in for a false notion of civility or, worse, the self-protection of leaders who'd rather get a slap on the back than an honest assessment? Those are the questions I'll seek to answer in the next chapter.

Notes

1. "Catholic Church Sexual Abuse Scandal: 7 Excerpts from the Grand Jury Report," accessed from www.nytimes.com/2018/08/14/us/catholic-priests-pennsylvania-church-jury.html.
2. James O'Toole and Warren Bennis, "A Culture of Candor," *Harvard Business Review*, June 2009.

Chapter 11

How to Let Your Light Shine

In his landmark book, *Good to Great*, Jim Collins describes his time with Vice Admiral James Stockdale—a naval aviator who spent eight years as a prisoner of war in Hanoi, North Vietnam. As the senior officer in his camp, Stockdale was forced to live in the paradoxical "darkness" of a solitary cell whose lights were kept on 24 hours a day as a form of psychological torture. Still, he survived. He fought back the false light of his tormentors with his own radical candor in coded letters sent to his wife, shared tactics for surviving torture, and improvised languages for communicating with his fellow captives.

The vast majority of us will never face anything even remotely like that, but we can learn something from Stockdale about candor, because the most striking element of his story is the power he found in confronting reality. While many of his fellow prisoners were "dying of a broken heart," he never allowed himself to shrink from the facts of his situation. Instead, he embraced reality. He told himself the truth about what was going on, and then he got to work on finding a way

DOI: 10.4324/9781003266556-11

to improve his and the others' situation. He found his power to influence fellow prisoners and help them through hell on earth not in candy-coating their predicament, but in telling them what they needed to hear in order to survive.

Candor Starts with Honesty about Ourselves

Candor is about brutal honesty; if we're not willing to get real with ourselves and others, we'll never truly grasp the Power of One. Note that I mentioned getting real *with ourselves*. One of the hardest things we can do is turn our gaze inward and get candid about what we see—to pluck the metaphorical log out of our own eye before we go looking for specks in others'. As hard as it is, this is step one in developing candor. If we don't get candid with ourselves, we can't expect anyone else to listen when we get candid with them. Worse, we won't allow ourselves to be confronted with the kind of truth we need to hear in order to become the best possible version of ourselves.

We're going to dwell on that last point, because it's only beginning to get the attention it deserves in our culture. On July 27, 2021, the world gasped in utter bewilderment when Simone Biles dropped out of the USA Gymnastics Team Final at the 2021 Summer Olympics in Tokyo.[1] Biles is a former gold winner for the U.S. and easily one of the greatest (if not *the* greatest) gymnasts alive. What led Biles to drop out? Was it an injury? The flu? COVID-19? None of the above. What side-lined Biles was her mental health and a genuine concern that her mind wasn't in a good place which, for a gymnast, could very easily represent a first-class ticket to serious injury.

Immediately following Biles' withdrawal, a flurry of criticisms spread across the internet. She was accused of folding under the pressure, abandoning her teammates, and letting her country down. None of this was fair, of course, but it's part of the territory when you're a professional athlete. Despite all the criticism, Biles stuck to her decision to protect her own mental and physical health. Within days, she had dropped out of the individual all-around and floor events, as well. She was candid with herself, even when the world was squeezing her to buck up and pretend like everything was okay. As a result of her candor, not only did she protect her own health, but she also set an example for athletes all over the world. It's okay to admit your limits and to gracefully step back for today in order to protect your tomorrow.

This message needs to be heard, not just in the world of athletics, but in workplaces as well. Some time ago, I heard a story (coincidentally, also out of Japan) that hammered this point home for me. In July 2013, a young journalist by the name Miwa Sado died of congestive heart failure in Tokyo. A 31-year-old journalist in the prime of her life, Sado's death was as unnecessary as it was tragic. What killed her? According to Japanese labor regulators, the cause of death was *karoshi*. No, that's not the Japanese word for some devastating illness—at least, not the kind of illness you might hear about in your general practitioner's office. *Karoshi* is the Japanese word for "death by work."

In the month prior to her death, Sado had logged nearly 160 hours of *overtime* with only two days off. That's 320 total hours of work in just one month! I'm sorry to say that this kind of workload is commonplace in Japan—even despite strict labor laws designed to curtail overwork and impose stiff fines on companies that try to squeeze too much out of their employees. As a result, *karoshi* is common as well. In 2016, nearly 1,500 instances of death by work were reported. The real number was certainly higher. Companies that have been found liable for *karoshi* deaths have had to pay out as much as 130 million YPD in damages to their victims' families. That's more than $1 million.

In Japan, *karoshi* isn't about greed or workaholism. It's about culture. Japanese companies are intensely hierarchical.

If you're low on the ladder, then you can expect to be treated like a nameless automaton whose sole purpose is to log as many hours as possible for the company. This kind of cultural malady is not at all limited to Japan. We may not literally work our employees to death, but I've been around plenty of corporate environments where the expectation was that junior employees would "pay their dues" by working 80-plus hours per week. For employees in circumstances such as these, the weight of their superiors' expectations is enough to keep them from ever fessing up to how tired and overwhelmed they are. Rather than being candid with themselves and their bosses, they continue to work themselves to the bone, sacrificing their physical, emotional, and relational health for the sake of an organization that sees them as little more than a productive worker bee.

We've all got to learn to stand up for our own health. We've got to cultivate the power to acknowledge our own limitations, not only to ourselves but to the people who expect us to do more than we can reasonably do. Trust me, it'll go far better for you if you walk into your boss's office and tell him he's overworking you than if you flame out and start calling in sick or dropping the ball at work. Like Simone Biles, we need to be willing to step back today in order to protect our tomorrow—even if it makes us feel like we're not living up to our potential or it ruffles a couple people's feathers. If Biles were reading this book, I bet she'd agree. And if Miwa Sado was still alive today, I'm sure she would agree as well.

Shining a Light on Our Privilege

Right now, our country is struggling to get honest with itself about the issue of privilege—social, cultural, racial, and otherwise. First, let's get something straight about the word *privilege*. When many people hear the word, they take it as something of a slur—a term of abuse that implies they haven't worked hard to get to where they are. Some people believe that privilege is reserved for white men born with a silver spoon in their mouths, but the truth of the matter is that we *all* have it in one way or another. Privilege is simply having an unearned advantage over someone else. I, for example, am privileged to have been born in a household with two college-educated parents. The unearned advantage there wasn't just that I was expected to go to college myself but that their personal experience equipped them to give me the guidance, resources, and tools I needed in order to get into a good school.

I never realized how significant privilege could be until I got to law school. You see, there weren't too many people who looked like me at my law school. There weren't too many single mothers there, either. Knowing how important the first semester of law school was for securing a summer clerkship and, eventually, a job, I worked my butt off to rank in the top of the class. As a result, I was invited to 15 interviews with firms. Afterward, I sat back and waited to see what firm I would be spending my summer with. Well, the first rejection letter came. Then, the fifth. Then, the tenth. Finally, the fifteenth rejection letter came. I was devastated! Meanwhile, I heard students in the bottom of the class brag about their summer clerkships. Many of them either had lawyers for parents or attorneys in their network who said, "All you have to do is graduate and pass the bar and you're guaranteed a job!" Talk about an unearned advantage!

The fact of the matter is that some members of our society begin this life with a leg up on their neighbors. In the case of my bottom-rung classmates, some start with *two* legs up! People can argue about whether that's fair or not and what should be done about it in terms of public policy, but what I'm most concerned with here is how we can *recognize* our privilege and what we can do with it. Don't think you're privileged?

Read the following list of statements and put a check by each one that applies to you:

- ■ English is my first language.
- ■ One or both of my parents graduated from college.
- ■ I've never had to skip a meal for lack of food in the house.
- ■ I have no disabilities.
- ■ I grew up in a family with health insurance.
- ■ I've never been bullied on account of my gender, ethnicity, or sexual orientation.
- ■ I am a citizen of the United States.
- ■ I come from a supportive family environment.
- ■ I've never been questioned by the police just because I looked suspicious.
- ■ I grew up with more than 50 books in my house.

How'd you do? If you find yourself with seven or more checkmarks, then you can consider yourself a fairly privileged individual. If you've got three or fewer, not so much.

Again, we can argue until we're blue in the face about whether any of this is just or unjust, but what we need to be concerned with right now are the brutal facts about the way things are and how we're going to respond as individual influencers. That said, if you do find yourself on the high end of the privilege spectrum, then you are in a position to leverage your unearned advantage not just for yourself but for those around you. Contrary to popular opinion, influence isn't about consolidating power and privilege. It's about sharing it. When you share your privilege with others, though, you don't really give it away. You only lend it, because in helping other people up to where you are, you empower them to help you climb even further. Then, in a virtuous cycle, you can pull them up once more. This is precisely what I was getting at earlier when I talked about "ourship." Together, we rise; divided, we fall.

What would it look like to lend your privilege instead of hoarding it for yourself and denying it to others? Here are three specific ways to leverage your unearned advantage for the sake of others:

1. **Lend your advocacy**. In the workplace, many people feel uncomfortable advocating for themselves due to systemic inequities. Perhaps you notice that your company does not allow leave for starting a non-traditional family. Although you may not need this type of leave, why not advocate for it because it's the right thing to do?

2. **Lend your credibility**. Some employees may be new to the organization or just haven't had the opportunity to gain credibility with all of the key players. If you have, then you have a unique opportunity to get to know these new employees and then invest your organizational capital in their growth. It's your name on the line, so you have to be wise, but generous investments such as these reap huge dividends as you usher valuable contributors into the inner circle.

3. **Lend your voice**. Many people do not have a voice in organizations but have meaningful contributions to share. Speaking up on behalf of the voiceless is an incredible way to lend your privilege and to ensure that the best ideas gain a hearing—regardless of where they've come from.

Recovering the Virtue of Candor

We all want to be like Stockdale—committed to speaking truth to ourselves and others no matter how brutal the facts may be. But we're afraid that, in our transparent honesty, we might . . .

- say the wrong thing.
- offend someone.
- tick off our boss.
- ruin a relationship.
- drive away a customer or a client.
- upset our spouse or partner.
- push away our children.
- confront our own fears.

These fears make sense. And, in a contentious world where people seem to be growing more and more sensitive to *anything* that smacks of incivility, we're right to be concerned about how our words will be received. But here are the facts on the ground:

- Others need our genuine feedback in order to become their best selves.
- Sometimes, we need to be "shook" in order to be awakened.
- Our bosses can't do their jobs unless we tell them what they need to know.
- You can't build a *true* relationship on eggshells and niceties.
- You'll never serve a client well by withholding the truth from them.
- If anyone deserves our candor, it's our spouse.
- Your kids need clarity and conviction more than a parent.

We need to speak the truth. We need to shine a light for the people around us to see. No matter what the pressure, we can't continue to withhold our candor for fear of ruffling feathers. We need to become the kind of people who don't quail under these pressures, but who clearly and confidently express the words that need to be said. This isn't so that we can tear people down, belittle, or hurt them, but so that, in the mutual interchange of open, honest feedback, we can all challenge one another to become the people we're meant to become. Through our candor, we can inspire one another to contribute in the ways we're meant to contribute and, together, to build our homes, communities, and organizations up into all that we know they can be. In a word, our world— from the people in our houses to the people on the streets— needs our *honesty*. They'll only get it if we recover the virtue of candor.

Practicing Virtue: How to Become a Candid Person

In Chapter 7, we saw the analogous relationship between hitting a major league fastball and cultivating the virtue of civility. The moral of that story was that, in the same way a hitter disciplines his body through countless hours or practice in the batting cage, we train ourselves to act with civility by stepping into the ordinary cage of life and swinging at every opportunity to be civil. In that way, we won't merely become people who do civil things; we'll become *civil people* who instinctively act with civility.

Candor is much the same. We don't become candid people by summoning up all our willpower in the morning and saying, "I'm going to be a candid person today!" No, we learn candor in the everyday grind of life with others. Every time we speak an honest word despite our fear and discomfort, we grow a little in our candor. Every time we resist the urge to say, "it's fine," and we tell someone how we really feel about the way they've made us feel, we take another step toward becoming candid people. In sum, candor takes *practice*. It takes a conscious effort to seize "little" opportunities for candor and use them to train ourselves in the way of honesty, authenticity, and transparency.

Ten Practices for Cultivating Candor

Here are 10 practices to take up as you seek to put on the
virtue of candor. Like I advised in Chapter 7, be sure to read
these practices each morning. Post them in a prominent
place and remind yourself of them throughout the day. Check
yourself in the evenings. How'd you do? What will you do to
improve the next day? Work these practices into your life until
they become reflexive habits. As you do, you'll become the
kind of person who gives candid feedback without hesitation.
More importantly, you'll become the kind of person others
want to listen to—in other words, a person of true influence.

1. **Invite real talk.** To give candor, you have to be willing
   to get candor. Invite others to speak clearly and directly
   into your life. By giving them that right, you'll earn *your*
   right to speak candidly with others.
2. **Receive feedback well.** When others *do* speak directly
   with you, make a concerted effort to receive that feedback
   in a positive light. Even if their words are harsh, seek the
   truth in their criticism and express appreciation for their
   words.
3. **Drop the euphemisms.** We all know that phrases such
   as "growth opportunities" are really code for "weakness."
   Pay attention to the soft words you use to tamp down the
   truth and replace them with more direct communication.
4. **Walk *toward* difficult conversations.** Candor can hurt,
   and our instinct is often to avoid moments when we
   know we'll have to give or receive hard words. Make an
   effort to move toward—not away—from those difficult
   moments.
5. **Start positive.** Season critical words with positivity. This
   isn't about sugar-coating; it's about encouraging. Find
   something to praise, emphasize it, and show how your
   criticism helps others live into the quality you flagged.

6. **Speak to build, not to tear down.** If the motivation behind a conversation is your desire to wound the other person or vent your frustration, then keep your peace. Candor without civility is just verbal harassment. It does no one any good.

7. **Keep it short.** The more words you use, the less likely it is that you're clearly getting to the heart of the matter. Don't dance around what you have to say; just say it in as clear and direct a manner as possible.

8. **Actively seek clarity.** No matter how clear you are, people hear things differently. Be sure to ask for feedback as you communicate; ask what they're hearing. Don't allow them the opportunity to misconstrue what you're saying.

9. **Excavate emotions.** Sparks might fly. If you're being candid with someone and they begin to react, ask why. Is it because you're being unkind or unfair, or because they're bumping up against an uncomfortable truth?

10. **Keep calm and candor on.** Speaking of emotions, it's important you keep your own in check. If you find yourself reacting emotionally to someone else's candor, ask yourself why. Which of your buttons are they pressing?

Conclusion

Many have said that stress doesn't build character; it reveals it. The "Hanoi Hilton" didn't *make* Stockdale an American hero; it merely *revealed* the hero that already dwelled within him. As we read earlier, that heroism depended on his ability to embrace the brutal facts of his imprisonment without losing his optimism. That paradox allowed him to become a person of true influence in that prison camp—to exercise his Power of One for the good of his fellow soldiers and sailors. The Medal of Honor that President Gerald R. Ford hung around

Stockdale's neck in 1976 was a testimony to the power of candor to look down the barrel of reality and refuse to blink.

You're probably not working in the Hanoi Hilton. But, if your experience is like that of an overwhelming majority of people in corporate America, then what your colleagues need more than anything is for you to embrace the reality of your situation and speak truth from that place. Shine a light. Become a person of candor, the "safe" person who others can rely on to always speak his or her mind—not out of anger or malice—but out of a sincere desire to see them and their organizations prosper. Be that person and you *will* influence others for the better. Candor is power, *your* power. Stop hiding it under the bushel of false civility and start using it to make this world a better place.

Note

1. Due to COVID-19 shutdowns, the 2020 games were held in 2021.

Chapter 12

Creating a Culture of Candor

In early 2018, Attorney General Jeff Sessions fired former FBI Deputy Director Andrew McCabe. Why? According to the Justice Department and the FBI, McCabe "lacked candor" in his discussions with investigators.[1] When pressed about some of the claims he made during the 2016 presidential election, it appears, McCabe tried to spin the facts in order to protect his career. Writing in *The Atlantic*, Adam Serwer reported that "candor violations" such as these are fairly common in the bureau: "one former FBI official estimated 20 to 30 bureau employees were dismissed annually for matters of candor."[2] If it's willing to give up 20 to 30 employees *every year*, one thing about the FBI is clear: they're not messing around with candor. Tell the truth or find another place to work.

According to a former agent interviewed by Serwer, candor violations are treated more harshly than other "more serious" violations (a DUI, for example). Why all the fuss about candor? Serwer's interviewee sheds a bit of helpful light: "'You have to be able to back up your statements, and if you don't have good candor, you can't go jamming people up for lying to federal

DOI: 10.4324/9781003266556-12

agents.'"[3] In other words, candor is essential to both the integrity and the efficacy of the FBI. Without it, individual agents won't be able to withstand scrutiny in the courtroom, and justice will ultimately suffer. The Bureau has no choice, then: maintain a culture of candor or give up the ability to do its job.

Woody, Buzz, and the Braintrust

In the private sphere, companies face a much different "legal" trial than that of the FBI: the court of public opinion. Here, we might take a cue from Pixar, whose many animated movies (*Toy Story, Cars, Up*, etc.) have come to dominate the cultural horizons of an entire generation (not to mention their parents). How is it that Pixar has been able to churn out one hit movie after another? How can this animation studio consistently pump out movies that feature brilliant animation *and* captivating storytelling? What's their secret, because I want to know!

In his 2014 book, *Creativity Inc.*, the former president of Pixar and Walt Disney Animation Studios, Ed Catmull, attributes the lion's share of Pixar's success to one thing: systematic candor.

> Candor is the key to collaborating effectively. . . . One of Pixar's key mechanisms is the Braintrust, which we rely on to push us toward excellence and to root out mediocrity. It is our primary delivery system for straight talk. . . . Its premise is simple: Put smart, passionate people in a room together, charge them with identifying and solving problems, and encourage them to be candid. The Braintrust is not foolproof, but when we get it right, the results are phenomenal.[4]

Pixar's Braintrust developed organically out of the original creative team behind *Toy Story*. When the creative process behind

Toy Story 2 began to flag, the studio took that organic relationship and created a system that continues today. According to Catmull, the candid feedback passed around the Braintrust makes Pixar's movies what they are:

> Candor could not be more crucial to our creative
> process. Why? Because early on, all of our movies
> suck. . . . I'm not trying to be modest or self-effacing.
> Pixar films are not good at first, and our job is to make
> them so—to go, as I say, "from suck to not-suck."[5]

As Catmull so helpfully explains, the road from "suck" to "not-suck" is paved with candor. By way of the Braintrust, everyone on the team is challenged to lay their own candid brick by giving and receiving honest feedback. The result? Great movies.

From Cartoons to Cultures

The candor of a Braintrust may sound good for creative outfits such as Pixar where collaboration seems to be a natural extension of who they are and what they do. What about a restaurant management company or an industrial manufacturer? As a structure, the Braintrust (or something like it) may not work in many environments, but that doesn't make its driving force (candor) any less pertinent to the "less creative" among us. As we've seen throughout this section of the book, candor is sorely lacking in all kinds of organizations. Every culture, big or small, can benefit from an uptick in honesty, transparency, and constructive truth-telling (i.e., civil candor).

In the previous chapter, we looked at how to become a candid individual. Here, we take that same idea and expand it out to the broader level. How do we bring candor into our homes, workplaces, and communities? How do we take our Power of One and become candid influencers, so much so that others see our light shining so brightly that they decide they want to join us? How do we create a space where others can genuinely feel free to communicate directly and openly without fear of offense or reprisal? Ultimately, these are questions of *culture*, and their answers require our intentional investment as we seek to multiply influence.

In the following, I organize my answers to these cultural questions around three words: model, invite, protect. Before I unpack them, though, I want you to remember that my advice isn't just for leaders. Sure, much of what I say will be geared for those who hold positional authority, but not exclusively so. You may not be able to create and implement a reward structure for candid feedback in your organization, but you can "reward" candor by receiving it well and expressing genuine appreciation for what others have to say—especially about you and your contribution to the team. You may not be able to control the dissemination of information in your company as a whole, but you can control the information under *your* purview, seeing to it that everyone around you knows what they need to know, when they need to know it. In sum, you can *lead* with candor from *wherever* you are. Through your example, you can start a revolution of candor that works its way through your culture from the ground up.

Now, when more and more Americans are waking up to systemic injustice in our nation, is the time for this revolution of candor. The darkened habits of far too many employers in corporate America have erected many barriers for underrepresented groups in the workplace. It's important we recognize that these habits aren't all rooted in conscious bigotry or bad will. In many cases, the opposite is the case. A study out of Cornell University, for example, shows that women are more likely than men to be lied to in performance reviews.[6] Nobody walks into those meetings saying to themselves, "I'm going to lie through my teeth." That's because these "little white lies" aren't meant to deceive so much as to protect women from the brutal truth. The intentions may be good, but the resulting lack of candor robs the woman in question of the feedback she needs in order to grow in her position. If we want to give women (or any other underrepresented group) the opportunity to succeed, we've got to respect them enough to be completely candid about their performance.

Model Candor

True leaders go first. They set the tone for others by modeling the behavior they want to see. Wherever you are on the totem pole, you *are* a leader (see Chapter 2). You have the power to influence others for the better and to show them what it looks like to embrace candor and leverage it for the good of everyone on the team. That said, begin with my advice in Chapter 11 and become a candid person. As you do, though, add in these intentional elements to take your candor public and create a revolution of candor in your workplace or community.

1. **Be predictable.** Tell the truth, and don't change your story just to suit your mood. According to James O'Toole and Warren Bennis, "Leaders who are candid and predictable . . . signal to followers that the rules of the game aren't changing and that decisions won't be made arbitrarily."[7] Not only will that inspire your people to do great work, but it'll encourage them to carry forward your example.

2. **Share your information.** Don't allow your workplace to become a mushroom farm. As far as you're able, open the books and invite your coworkers to see *exactly* how the sausage is made—all the way down to the grubbiest detail.

3. **Critique the wins and the losses.** When Sheryl Sandberg addressed Kim Scott's "um" problem, she didn't do it after a loss. She did it after a *win*, refusing to let

momentary success blind her to the fixes that needed to be made to ensure long-term sustainability. Critiquing your wins helps in that endeavor. It also creates a more receptive environment for when you need to critique a loss.

Invite Candor

If modeling is the foundation of cultural candor, then invitation is its structure. Inviting candor is about more than asking a colleague into your office to tell you how they think your last presentation went. It's about creating both an environment and a structure in which candor can be systematically encouraged and given every opportunity to flow freely from top to bottom, bottom to top.

1. **Allow people to get real.** This may sound simplistic, but people need permission to speak freely—not a feckless invitation to "let us know if you have any concerns" but a genuine invitation for candid communication. This begins with modeling (see the previous section), but it only gets off the ground if leaders turn to their people and encourage them to offer direct feedback without fear of reprisal.
2. **Get candid about candor.** Often hailed as "the CEO of the 20th century," Jack Welch has had much to say about the power of candor in the workplace. According to a 1984 article in *Fortune*, however, Welch didn't exactly encourage his people to challenge him: "Welch conducts meetings so aggressively that people tremble. He attacks almost physically with his intellect—criticizing, demeaning, ridiculing, humiliating." If you want to encourage candor, don't penalize people when they get candid with you.
3. **Encourage contrarians**. O'Toole and Bennis tell the story of a young manager at Motorola in the 1980s. When

he approached then-CEO Robert Galvin and said, "Bob, I heard that point you made this morning, and I think you're dead wrong," the CEO didn't bristle. Instead, he turned to a colleague and declared, "That's how we've overcome Texas Instruments' lead in semiconductors!"[8] Contrarian's force leaders to stay on top of their game; contrarians encourage complacency.

Protect Candor

A candid culture is only as strong as the support its people are willing to lend to it. If you invite candor, but fail to protect the people under your care, you'll end up ushering in more darkness than before. Use the following suggestions to help you create and maintain a safe environment for candor.

Create Venues for Candor

Pixar's Braintrust is a great example of a venue where people can expect to give and receive candor. The video analytics company Hudl did something similar by creating a card game in which each card included candor-inviting instructions such as, "Tell the person on your left one thing they can improve on," or "Give us an example of something someone did that disappointed you."[9] Whether it's a braintrust, a game, or a feedback session, creating these "safe zones" for candor will not only encourage real talk (see earlier discussion), but it'll communicate that candor is valued and that you're willing to protect those who speak their mind.

Develop Relationships

Strong relationships built on authentic connections are ultimately the best venue for candor because we're far more willing to receive feedback from the people we know, love, and trust. When we know that the person speaking hard truth to us is committed to our success, we're eager to hear what they have to say about how we can do better. Where no such trust exists, our guard goes up and we enter into defense mode. Additionally, relationships carry within them their own organic accountability structures. In the ordinary course of life and work together, friends do a much better job of negotiating the fine line between civil and uncivil candor than policies and procedures ever could.

Establish Guidelines

Though they may ultimately work better at protecting candor, relationships are no substitute for policies and procedures. Save your employees the trouble of having to figure out what constitutes acceptable vs. unacceptable candor. In tandem with your "civil constitution" (see Chapter 8), develop a set of guidelines laying out appropriate and inappropriate versions of real talk. Be sure to convey that the purpose of candor isn't to tear down others but to contribute to the good of the individual and the organization.

Expect the Truth

One of the best ways to protect the light is to show zero tolerance for darkness. As part of your guideline document, lay out the consequences for those who either withhold information or willingly misinform others. Commit to transparency and make it clear that you're not willing to tolerate anything less.

Inequities

Acknowledge that not everyone is participating on a level playing field. Systemic inequities have contributed to many people being marginalized in the workplace. Acknowledging this truth and being candid about how the systems and processes in your organization have perpetuated these inequities is a crucial way to begin creating an equitable workplace.

The Promise of a Candid Culture at Work and in the Community

No culture exists for the sake of itself. Families exist to love, support, and encourage one another to thrive in life. Neighborhoods exist to foster warmth, connection, and community. Non-profits exist to serve the world. Businesses exist to do the same, but to make money as they do. Nations—at least, the good ones—exist to safeguard the interests of their citizens and promote their flourishing. Without candor, these cultures fail to live up to their charter; they create citizens who care more about their own needs than those of everyone around them. When this happens, it's only a matter of time before the darkness creeps in and wreaks havoc on what was once a vibrant, beautiful institution.

With candor, family members embrace the freedom to speak the hard words that often need to be spoken. With candor, neighbors reach across the metaphorical fences that divide and create meaningful relationships through honest dialogue. With candor, non-profits confront and overcome the brutal realities of trying to run an organization on a shoestring budget. With candor, businesses clear out the darkness that infiltrates and obstructs what would otherwise be a smooth operation. With candor, citizens engage in open dialogue with one another, but they do it from a desire to see nations thrive and individuals flourish. This is what candor has to offer us if only we'd give ourselves and others the freedom to shine our light in humble confidence that, together, we can make a better world.

In Chapter 6, we talked about microaggressions and how they create a culture in which minority groups are made to feel inferior to others. What would change in these workplaces if organizational citizens spoke candidly about the microaggressive words and actions they witnessed in the workplace? What would happen if victims and witnesses alike spoke up against the aggressors, letting them know about the specific ways in which their words caused harm? You might lick your chops at the idea of putting an insensitive ignoramus in his place, but what if these acts of candor accomplished something even better? What if, in engaging the aggressors with candor, you helped them arrive at a new level of understanding? What if your candor was able to open up a genuine dialogue and create a new sense of mutual respect and common vision? Therein lies the true cultural promise of candor. When we engage each other with the truth in a respectful way, we don't just win arguments or convince the other person how wrong they are. We grow *together* and pave a better path toward the future.

Conclusion: A Plea for Candor

After a grand jury decided not to indict police officer Darren Wilson in the 2014 shooting of Michael Brown, the then chairman and CEO of Kaiser Permanente, the late Bernard Tyson, took to LinkedIn to advocate for a revolution in race relations.[10] As a Black leader, he saw it as his duty to change the narrative around race. To create the change we all want to see, he said, "we have to tell the truth." He was right. The only way cultures change for the better is when their citizens speak up and speak out.

What would change if we decided to put down our sense of relational comfort and pick up candor? How would our workplaces change if we became radical truth speakers? What kind of influence would we enjoy if our friends, neighbors, and coworkers began to lean on us for advice, all because they *knew* we would respond with the honest words they know they need to hear? How would our companies improve if we all agreed to make the workplace a safe place for the unvarnished truth? Imagine the flourishing we could see in our homes, workplaces, and communities when we drop the pretense and pick up candor.

As I've argued throughout this chapter, the personal and corporate benefits of candor are immense. If we want to become people of influence who use our Power of One to benefit others, we have to become truth-tellers. We have to realize that the most civil thing we can do, in most cases, is to deliver the unadulterated truth to our fellow citizens— at home, in the office, or out in the community. To do that, though, we need more than just civility and candor. We need courage—lots of it.

Notes

1. Matt Zapotosky, "Andrew McCabe, Trump's Foil at the FBI, is Fired Hours Before He Could Retire," *Washington Post*, March 17, 2018.
2. Adam Serwer, "Why the FBI Fires People for 'Lack of Candor'," *The Atlantic*, March 22, 2018.
3. Clint Watts, cited in Ibid.
4. Ed Catmull, "Inside the Pixar Braintrust," *Fast Company*, excerpt from Creativity Inc., accessed October 6, 2021 from www.fastcompany.com/3027135/inside-the-pixar-braintrust.
5. Ibid.
6. Vivan Zayas and Lily Jampol, "Gendered White Lies: Women Are Given Inflated Performance Feedback Compared to Men," *Psy Ar Xiv*, September 22, 2020, accessed October 6, 2021 from https://psyarxiv.com/yq24b/.
7. James O'Toole and Warren Bennis, "A Culture of Candor," *Harvard Business Review*, June 2009.

8. Ibid.
9. *Real Talk Blog*, accessed from https://zapier.com/blog/real-talk-hudl-company-culture/.
10. Bernard J. Tyson, "It's Time to Revolutionize Race Relations," *LinkedIn*, December 4, 2014, accessed October 6, 2021 from www.linkedin.com/pulse/20141204174020-261404895-it-s-time-to-revolutionize-race-relations/.

Chapter 13

What Is Courage?

On May 25, 2020, a Black man named George Floyd was murdered unjustly at the hands of a white police officer in Minneapolis. The entire incident was captured on video and posted, creating an instantaneous backlash. Immediately, people across the country took to the streets in protest. On Twitter, citizens cried out for justice. *Forbes'* Mike Federle quickly became the first CEO of a major organization to publicly declare: "Black Lives Matter." Plenty more followed suit after him. Other leaders matched their words with actions, actively laying down their privilege in efforts to elevate the marginalized as a beautiful act of what I've called "ourship." As I mentioned earlier in the book, Reddit co-founder Alexis Ohanian resigned from the company's board after 15 years of service to make room for a person of color.[1]

In Federle and Ohanian, we see two high-profile acts of the ingroup (the majority) geared toward advancing the interests of the outgroup (minorities). But these final chapters aren't so much about those prominent acts of courage you see on TV or that are plastered across social media. Much closer to home, these final chapters focus on the ordinary,

DOI: 10.4324/9781003266556-13

everyday courage that comes from the Power of One. It's the courage an insider shows when he sacrifices a measure of his own privilege in order to elevate an overlooked outsider in the workplace. It's the bravery summoned up by a member of the community who's willing to stand up for the justice of her neighbors. It's the grit to speak truth to power, no matter how difficult it may be. And, while we're thankful for the Federles and Ohanians who exercise their Power of One on the national corporate stage, it's the exercise of this ordinary, everyday courage by individuals at every level of culture that will ultimately make the world a much better place for everyone.

Courage: A Matter of the Heart

In these final chapters of the book, we're going to focus on the third and final C of influence: courage. What comes to mind when you hear the word *courage*? Do you envision a firefighter running into a burning building? Or maybe you see a soldier marching off into battle? You might think of one of Harvey Weinstein's outspoken victims, risking her career to put a monster behind bars. The fact is that courage takes many forms:

- The son who tells his father he's transitioning.
- The daughter who is depressed and admits she needs help.
- The teenager who refuses to follow his friends down dangerous paths.
- The employee who marches up to his boss and asks for a raise.
- The ex-employee who won't compromise her principles for the sake of a job.

- The leader who stands up in front of a crowd and admits they've done wrong.
- The CEO who says, "Black Lives Matter."
- The board member who gives up his own seat to make room for others.

The word *courage* traces back to the Latin word *cor,* which means "heart." The heart has long been considered the metaphorical seat, sum, and center of human existence. In the Bible, for example, Proverbs 4:23 says, "Above all else, guard your *heart,* for everything you do flows from it." In older English, "courage" got at that idea, meaning something like "what's in your heart." Back then, it was possible to have good or bad courage—depending, of course, on your disposition. Today, courage means something much more specific. It's not just about what's in your heart; it's about the *strength* of what's in your heart. When someone acts in a cowardly way, we describe them as "faint of heart." When we want to encourage someone, we tell them to "take heart." Of course, how many young men have grown up with a vision of courage modeled for them in the movie *Braveheart?* For our purposes, then, let's define courage as "the strength of heart to act on what you know to be right."

Sometimes, people understand courage to mean action *without* fear, but that's not quite right. Courage isn't the absence of fear. Rather, it's the absence of the *wrong kinds* of fear and the presence of the *right* fear in the *right* proportion. A courageous person, for example, may be afraid of making a fool of himself in a presentation, but he gets up and gives the presentation anyway. In right measure, that kind of fear is good—it will help him to keep from procrastinating, do his preparation, and pay careful attention to his delivery. The absence of that fear wouldn't make him more courageous— it'd make him foolish. Similarly, a courageous soldier may be

afraid to die, but she's *more afraid* of letting down her unit
or causing one of her fellow soldier's harm. So, she steels her
nerves, remembers her training, and runs into the firefight
rather than away from it.

Courage and the Power of One

I've saved courage for the final chapters of this book, not
because it's the least important of the three C's but because,
without courage, the other two simply don't get off the
ground. It takes courage to sacrifice your interests for the good
of the whole (civility). It takes courage to walk up to another
person and tell them the uncomfortable truth (candor). It takes
courage to look at the world around you—whether it's a toxic
office culture, a turbulent home, a racist system, or a contentious neighborhood—and pursue the uncomfortable path of
positive influence. It takes courage to look deep within, locate
your Power of One, and resolve to bring it out into the world
for the good of others.

The Power of One is never easy. Remember the cardiac
nurse who ignored her boss and peers to give my mother a
hearing and, eventually, set me on a course to full health?
How about Harold Cottam and the way he bucked the chain
of command to report *Titanic*'s distress? Or, how about James
Stockdale and the candor he embraced in Hanoi? It would've
been easier for my nurse to hang up the phone, but then I
wouldn't still be around to write this book. It would have
been far less dangerous for his career if Cottam just went to
bed, but how many *more* people would've frozen to death? It
would have been safer for Stockdale to keep his head down
and wait things out, but how many more of his fellow prisoners would've died of a broken heart? The Power of One takes
courage. Without it, who knows what important work we'll
leave undone?

The Workplace Needs Our Courage

Thanks, in large part, to the events of 2020, more and more organizations have finally found the courage to proclaim from the rooftops what was once only whispered among a small minority of social activists: Black Lives Matter. On the one hand, this is a statement of solidarity—a verbal locking-of-the-arms with all who've had to live with the unjust killing of Black men, women, and children at the hands of biased police officers across America. On the other hand, this is an organizational call to action. Within corporate America, the statement "Black Lives Matter" has signaled a commitment to address the long-standing racial inequities that have plagued the workplace for decades.

Let's not be naïve. Some of these voices are fair-weather friends, interested less in social change and more in winning new business or avoiding the tremendous backlash their silence would invite, not just from their Black employees, but from their clients, stakeholders, and customers as well. They may become allies for a time, but they'll never truly see this as "our" ship, and it won't be long before their courage fails and they heed the siren song of the status quo. Thankfully, there are plenty of signs to indicate that, for the most part, corporate proponents of racial justice are doing so in good faith. This excerpt of an email from Anna Wintour, Editor-in-Chief of *Vogue* magazine, is one of those signs:

> I want to start by acknowledging your feelings and expressing my empathy towards what so many of you are going through: sadness, hurt, and anger too. . . .

> I want to say this especially to the Black members of our team—I can only imagine what these days have been like. But I also know that the hurt, and violence, and injustice we're seeing and talking about

have been around for a long time. Recognizing it and doing something about it is overdue.[2]

Like Wintour and *Vogue*, many organizations have openly admitted that they'd created systems of inequities that left their Black employees behind without any real hope for advancement. They've paid Black workers less, denied them titles and power, and held them back from more desirable work. They've also turned their back on the everyday injustices that can permeate the workplace: exclusion, harassment, marginalization, microaggression. To confess these cultural sins was to take on great social *and* legal risk. Customers could've balked and Black employees could've easily leveraged these statements as evidence to sue their employers for racial discrimination. But, to my knowledge, none have. Why? Because of the promise and reward of courage. Corporate America has stuck its neck out and pledged to make things right. Black employees are jumping at this opportunity to claim their rightful place, not by litigious force, but through their own display of courage, trust, and hope for a better tomorrow.

As we consider the promise of courage, I invite you to envision what that better tomorrow would look like. What would change for us and the people around us if we were to recover the virtue of courage and empower others to do the same? What kind of person would *you* become if you were to find the courage to do what you've always known you needed to do but couldn't find it in you to do it? What would change if we could summon up the courage to:

■ Admit that our organizations have been operating in default mode when it comes to racial, social, economic, and other injustices within our culture.
■ Commit to doing better by identifying blind spots and developing strategic solutions for leveling the playing field.

- Listen to the people who've been hurt by giving them a safe space to air their grievances.
- Cut loose those leaders who've refused to own up to their role in creating a hostile, intimidating work environment for underrepresented groups.
- Put value on our values by refusing to work with those clients and customers whose toxic cultural commitments threaten to bring harm to our own people.

Conclusion

Although many organizations have begun to work overtime to dismantle inequitable work environments, there remains much to be done at every level of corporate America. Women in general are being treated with more respect than before, but there are still plenty of minority voices in the workplace who've not yet been heard. People of color are *slowly* being given a seat at the table, but the upper echelons of power have a long way to go before they fully reflect the diversity that has made our country so great. I'm confident that we'll get there, but we're not going to arrive at our destination without having to do some very hard work.

The death of George Floyd and the resulting cries for justice have made us all more sensitive to the many injustices that our marginalized neighbors have to face on a daily basis. For all but the most hardened, we are seeing new opportunities to address these issues together. We need the Mike Federles of the world to speak up for justice and the Alexis Ohanians to embody ourship by laying down their own privilege for the sake of others. But more than high-profile support, we need a revolution and recovery of courage from top to bottom. True and lasting change will only come when we *all* tap into our Power of One and start doing our part to save our sinking ship. In these final chapters of the book, I hope to help you do just that.

Notes

1. Isabel Togoh, "Michael Seibel Becomes Reddit's First Black Board Member after Alexis Ohonian's Resignation," *Forbes Magazine*, June 10, 2020, accessed from www.forbes.com/sites/isabeltogoh/2020/06/10/michael-seibel-becomes-reddits-first-black-board-member-after-alexis-ohanians-resignation/#79cc1e0a430a.
2. Leanne Italie, "Anna Wintour Apologize for Race-related 'Mistakes'," *ABC News: Business,* June 10, 2020, accessed from https://abcnews.go.com/Business/wireStory/anna-wintour-apologizes-race-related-mistakes-71179515.

Chapter 14

The Curse of a Faint Heart

As a human resources professional, I wasn't exactly surprised by the Harvey Weinstein scandal or the countless stories of racism in the workplace after the death of George Floyd. These stories were not new to me. In fact, I was often the first person a victim would approach for advice. From their very first day on the job, employees knew that when I said, "zero tolerance for harassment and discrimination," I meant it. I wasn't about to let misconduct go unchecked on my watch, and I certainly wasn't going to let one of our employees have their rights and dignity trampled over.

Thanks to my training in law, I knew precisely how to substantiate a harassment claim. After my due diligence was done, I would put on my lawyer hat and lay out my arguments before the senior leadership. In each case, I'd start by appealing to their sense of self-interest. Harassment, bullying, and intimidation would not only cost the organization in terms of legal fees; they'd also contribute to low productivity, employee disengagement, and a rotten corporate culture. After making the case for zero tolerance, I'd go on to show why the

DOI: 10.4324/9781003266556-14

perpetrator in question had truly committed wrongdoing and needed to be dealt with in no uncertain terms.

I was good at what I did, and if the wrongdoer had really done wrong, I made it crystal clear to everyone in the room why it was in everyone's best interest that they act decisively. About 99% of the time, my arguments did what they were supposed to do—expose the truth and facilitate the appropriate corrective action. As soon as the leadership saw there was wrongdoing, they acted swiftly and decisively on my recommendation. This is how things should work in civil organizations where candor is valued and leaders have the courage to do the right thing no matter the cost.

You'll notice I said 99%. I'm haunted by that remaining 1%—those few-yet-pivotal cases where leadership *didn't* take action. Why did they not act on my recommendations? Was it because I had failed to make my case? Was it because they knew some set of important exculpatory facts that I didn't? I *wish* I could chalk those instances up to my own failure or their better judgment, but the sad reality is that these leaders *knew* I was right, and they had no good reason to think otherwise. Yet even though they knew that workplace misconduct had taken place, they chose not to follow my recommendations. The question remains, then: *why* would a leader choose to ignore a clear instance of wrongdoing and carry on as though it had never happened?

Leading from Fear

Most organizations have what I like to call their "highly valued employees." They're the "superstar," the "rainmaker," or the "closer." They bring prime value to the organization, so they tend to get a pass. Never mind the people they hurt and the disengagement and resentment they breed throughout the organizations. Nobody wants to kill the golden goose, and plenty of them justify protecting him or her by pointing to their vital contribution to the organization. Then, they discredit, ignore, or pay off accusers to avoid having to discipline their top producers and threaten their bottom line.

Say what you want about corporate greed or favoritism. Although those elements are certainly in play when leadership fails to root out misconduct, I believe there's a more primal emotion behind this failure to hold high-value employees accountable: fear. To put it baldly, leaders are reluctant to discipline their star players because they're afraid of the consequences. They're afraid that . . .

■ they'll make the wrong call.
■ productivity will fall through the floor.
■ the company will tank.
■ terminated employees will join up with a competitor.
■ other high-value employees will lose their faith and trust in management.

These fears are understandable, but they're shortsighted. They welcome the short-term boon of a rainmaker at the expense of the organization's long-term health. Worse, they make it plain for everyone involved that the company values its profitability more than the physical and psychological safety of its employees. From an engagement perspective, that's a terrible way to attract and retain quality talent. Legally speaking, it invites costly litigation down the road. Whichever way you slice it, cowardice is more than just a bad look for companies; it's a disease that will ruin them from the inside. As I said in the previous chapter, courageous leaders don't have to pretend these fears don't exist. What they *need* is to do is summon the nerve to do the right thing whether they're afraid or not.

Leading with Fear

To combat the cowardice that lets abusers hurt others with impunity, leaders need a strong dose of courage. Unfortunately, many leaders trade genuine bravery for its red-headed step-cousin: bravado. Bravado is *faux* courage—it puts on a strong show, but all that courageous front does is mask deep-seated insecurity and cowardice. We see it in movies all the time: the work or school bully (think: Biff Tanen in *Back to the Future*) puts on a brave front but cowers in the face of real danger, only to have the runt (George McFly) swoop in to demonstrate real courage. In its worst form, bravado is at such pains to avoid a fearful appearance that it actually *uses* fear to its own ends. Like the schoolyard bully, it builds itself up by tearing others down.

At the individual level, people who lead with fear use implicit and explicit threats to cajole others into doing their bidding. A good example of an implicit threat would be the restaurant manager who only awards the best shifts to those servers who stay on her good side. Here's another example: if your manager has a penchant for losing his cool, then you might work under the implicit threat of being humiliated for your next mistake. Explicit threats are much more straightforward: "Screw up again, and I'll have your job." In either case, the primary motivator isn't a desire to see the organization succeed; it's fear.

In a culture where fear is used as a weapon, you can expect to find little to no civility or candor. The former evaporates as employees take up blame-shifting as a means of self-protection and rely on office political allegiances as a source of job security. Candor fizzles when employees withhold crucial feedback for fear of rejection, reprisal, or relational friction. Creativity wanes as employees learn to "play it safe" for fear of making costly mistakes. When everyone feels like they're living on the edge, no one can feel free to do their best work. Fear may be effective at keeping everyone in line, but the price of conformity is a bland, lifeless workplace that falls far short of its true potential.

The Personal and Professional Cost of Cowardice

How do you quantify a lack of courage in terms of cost to the organization? One of the simplest ways to do that is to look at the potential legal fees that can rack up when a particular instance of misconduct isn't handled appropriately or a hiring/ firing decision is made for the wrong reasons. Defending a company against an employment lawsuit can range from $125,000 (summary judgment) to $250,000 (jury trial) and beyond (depending on damages). Many organizations, of course, will choose to settle outside of court in order to defray some—not all—of those costs. When you factor in multiple offenses, those numbers can add up very quickly. But even if a company doesn't have to go to court and pay out in terms of dollars and cents, they'll still have to pay the price for their institutional cowardice in the form of increased employee absence, related turnover, and a drop in productivity for every-one involved in the dispute.

The steep financial costs that rack up when cultures lack courage easily grab our attention, but what about the *human* cost of cowardice? How do you put a price tag on the young mother who chooses to take her own life because her com-pany lacked the courage to stand up for her? How can we possibly calculate the deadening effect of an office culture where employees are forced to spend every moment grinding under the weight of fear-mongering leaders? It's high time we envision a culture where, instead of being manipulated by fear to *meet* expectations, employees are inspired to *exceed* them. But we'll never get there unless courageous leaders like you embrace their Power of One and exercise it for the sake of others.

So far, we've spent plenty of time on the organizational costs of fear and cowardice. But this book isn't primarily about the workplace so much as it's about *your* place at work and beyond. So, what does it cost *us* when we lack courage in our personal lives? As individuals, some of our deepest regrets are born out of those moments in which we lacked the courage to do what we knew was right:

- ■ "I should've said something."
- ■ "I shouldn't have let her leave."
- ■ "I wish I'd stepped in earlier."
- ■ "I never should've waited."
- ■ "I can't believe I let that stand."

As parents, friends, neighbors, and coworkers, we are faced with countless opportunities to show courage every day. From the performance review to the personal intervention, the people in our lives need our courage more than we could ever imagine. Sometimes, we need to stand up *for* them. Other times, we need to stand up *to* them. Either way, opportunities for genuine influence rarely show up apart from the need to exercise courage in some way. We will never discover and deploy our Power of One so long as we live in and lead from fear.

Conclusion

As I said in the previous chapter, courage is not the absence of fear. Rather, it's the strength to act in the face of fear. It makes perfect sense to worry about what might happen if a top producer leaves the company. What *doesn't* make sense is the decision to shield that high-value employee from appropriate discipline for misconduct. Decisions such as these reflect a deep-seated fear that cannot help but filter its way throughout the organization. The human price cowardly organizations such as these pay in terms of employee disengagement is beyond measure. Of course, that's not to mention the financial price they're having to pay when the penetrating light of the #MeToo movement exposes organizational cowardice and brings abusers to justice.

Whether we inhabit a role of positional leadership or not, it's up to us to counteract the pervasive cowardice that threatens to ruin our homes, offices, and neighborhoods. If we want to be powerful people of influence, we cannot tolerate the kind of cowardly behavior that lets abuse go overlooked. Nor can we settle for bravado as a cheap substitute for courage. No, we need the real deal—the strength of character and will to do what we know is right regardless of the consequences. It's time we find out how.

Chapter 15

The Firm Handshake

For years, I had coached hiring managers on what to look for in an ideal candidate: nice, polished dress; solid eye contact; a firm handshake. I also practiced what I preached, looking for these attributes in the candidates that I would interview and hire. A few years back, though, I had a hiring experience that completely changed the way I thought about these attributes. I had a position to fill—one that would report directly to me. After reviewing a stack of resumes, one candidate jumped out at me above all the others. When it came time to interview him, though, he defied my expectations in a way that made me question whether all those years I'd been looking for the wrong stuff in a new hire.

As I entered the room and reached out my hand for that all-important shake, the candidate pulled back: "Do you mind if I don't shake your hand?" I agreed to his polite request, of course, but from that point forward I couldn't stop thinking about it. Was there something wrong with me? Did my hand look dirty? Was it because I'm Black? I couldn't focus on a thing he had to say. I had tuned out of the interview and into my own curiosity about why this person would withhold what I took to be a crucial sign of civility and respect. But then,

DOI: 10.4324/9781003266556-15　　　　　　　　　　**139**

he came to a section of his resume in which there'd been a one-year gap. He explained to me that he'd suffered greatly from Rheumatoid Arthritis and that this year was bad enough to keep him out of work. Then, of course, came the follow-up: "That's why I couldn't shake your hand."

That moment triggered for me a significant reevaluation of everything I'd come to believe about evaluating candidates and employees on the basis of these largely superficial markers. Why did it matter if someone gave me a firm handshake? What did that really have to do with their ability to perform? And what about eye contact? I've known people on the autism spectrum who do excellent work yet feel incredibly uncomfortable making eye contact. Would it be fair for me to penalize them for that? Would I deprive myself of an excellent employee by making a mountain out of a molehill? Questions such as these began to unravel my expectations.

In the name of "professionalism," I'd taken my subjective pet peeves and projected them onto candidates as though they were scientific, objective criteria. I became my own version of that boss I mentioned earlier who assumed that, because I wore my natural curls to work one day, I must not have had any important meetings. Coming to this realization was painful; it required me to challenge my perception of what I'd always considered to make for a "quality" candidate or employee. I had to think deeply about the hidden biases and stereotypes that led me here, as well as what I would have to do to leave them behind. In sum, I had to admit that *I was wrong* so that I could get onto the right path. That kind of thing is never easy. For all of us, it takes courage.

The Three Traits of a Courageous Leader

I've told plenty of stories in this book, and I'm sure more than a few of them have hit home. The reality I've experienced in working with corporate leaders, though, is that a precious few are truly willing to change on the basis of what they've learned. It doesn't matter how many stories you've told and how many heads have nodded in response; the default mode is like quicksand. Escape is never easy and, if you're not careful, it'll swallow you up whole. Leaders who successfully imbibe the truth and overcome the law of inertia generally share these three traits:

1. **They invite authenticity**. It can be terrifying to let employees show up with true authenticity. I'm often asked what it would mean for me to be my authentic self at work. Does that mean I show up in my PJs and hair rollers? Of course not! Authenticity means you, as an employee, assimilate to corporate norms without leaving behind your unique identity. You don't change your name because it's too hard to pronounce. You don't modify your accent because you (or others) think it makes you sound stupid. You don't downplay your knowledge or expertise to make others feel more comfortable. Courageous leaders champion this kind of authenticity. Why? Because they're not looking for folks to conform to superficial cultural expectations. They're looking for people who add value.

2. **They welcome feedback.** Many leaders believe that feedback conversations only go one way. Nothing could be farther from the truth. Courageous leaders are not afraid to ask their employees questions such as "How am I doing?" or "What can I do to make your job easier?" or "What barriers am I putting in your way?" Those aren't hard questions to ask, but the answers can be incredibly hard to hear. You may not get authentic answers right away, especially if your team doesn't understand or trust your motives. But, once they see that you genuinely want feedback and want to use it in a positive way, they will begin to open up.

3. **They consistently hold others accountable**.
   Courageous leaders hold every single person to the same
   level of accountability. As I've mentioned several times in
   this book, too many people get a free pass when it comes
   to misbehavior. Although there are plenty of "explanations" for why companies do this, the fact is that there is
   no excuse. When it comes to showing dignity, respect,
   and honor, no one in your organization can be more
   worthy than anyone else. When I look back to the heart
   surgery that saved my life, I can't help but think past the
   cardiologist who performed the surgery to all the support
   staff who played a crucial role in my healing: the nurse
   who got me the appointment; the housekeepers who
   faithfully cleaned my room to stave off the threat of infection; the patient transport person who was just as excited
   as I was to see me go home. I may not remember their
   names, but I'll never forget what they did for me. They
   were indispensable; without them, that highly trained cardiologist would've been useless.

We are all leaders, whether we hold a title or not. A courageous person, whether she's "in leadership" or not, will leave
her metaphorical armor at the door as she engages in difficult
conversations that demand true authenticity from her and her
people. She'll speak hard truths, even as she invites others
to speak clearly and candidly with her. She will set aside the
broken narratives she's hidden behind and will hold herself
accountable (with everyone else) to the reality she discovers
around her. She will lead with the courage to challenge her
and others' misguided expectations and to instigate change
wherever it is needed.

Companies, neighborhoods, and community organizations
desperately need leaders like that, and the power is within
you to become one of them. All that's needed is for you to
acknowledge whatever level of influence you've been given

and to muster up the courage to wield that influence for the sake of others.

Recovering the Virtue of Courage

Many of us are ready to charge into battle no matter how scared we might be to fight injustice in the workplace. We *want* to become the kind of people who live into our values, speak with candor, and rise beyond the limitations of negative self-talk. We want this not only because it'll make *us* better, but because we know that cultivating the courage to deploy our inner power will be good for others as well. But for those of us who've spent so much time in the shadows, we're wondering: how do we develop that courage?

In previous chapters, I've argued that cultivating virtue isn't a matter of consciously engaging in the right behavior but of becoming the kind of person who unconsciously reacts to the world out of his or her virtuous heart. In that sense, becoming a courageous person doesn't mean responding to every situation by asking, "What would a courageous person do?" Instead, it looks a whole lot more like painstakingly developing a courageous habit of life. Step by step, through one small act of bravery after another, you can *grow* in courage. This doesn't happen all at once, and some find it easier than others. Nevertheless, courage is a virtue that we can *all* develop if we just devote ourselves to intentional practice.

Take the U.S. Army, for example. When soldiers from virtually every background you can think of show up at boot camp, a scant few of them have any real sense of what courage truly entails. They've never been to war, yet somehow, they need to develop the heart to run into battle and face the enemy head-on. How can they possibly do that? The answer is hard but simple: training (i.e., practice). After weeks of intensive training and countless opportunities to approach new challenges bravely, these soldiers develop a courageous habit—a new disposition that drives them to respond with instinctive bravery whenever the situation demands it. The Army is one of the best organizations in the world at cultivating this sort of virtue, and it shows as much in the many acts of bravery our servicemen and -women exhibit every day.

Practicing Virtue: How to Become a Courageous Person

In Chapter 13, I described courage as a matter of the heart. In this chapter, we're trying to "strengthen" the heart. How can you do that? The same way you'd strengthen your actual heart. As I've shared throughout this book, virtues such as civility, candor, and courage don't just happen. They're the product of continual habits and practices that train our hearts, minds, and bodies to respond rightly to the moment. A civil person treats her coworkers with dignity and respect because it doesn't occur to her to do otherwise. A candid person speaks the truth because he's learned to let his light shine by default. Likewise, a courageous person acts in the face of uncertainty and fear because she's stepped onto the treadmill of life, cranked up the speed, and trained herself to stand up instead of shrinking back—no matter what.

Ten Practices for Cultivating Courage

If you want to become a genuinely courageous person—the kind of friend, spouse, coworker, or leader who never lets fear stop him or her from doing the right thing—then the following 10 practices are for you. Courage isn't an innate gift; it's a virtue and a skill to be cultivated through intentional training.

By forcing you to seize everyday moments for bravery, the following practices will train you to instinctively choose the way of courage over the way of fear. As with the practices I shared in previous chapters, challenge yourself to read these practices every morning. Post them where you can see them and revisit your list throughout the day. At the end of each day, take a look at your list, assess how you did, and ask yourself (or, if you really want to be courageous, ask others) how you can do better tomorrow.

1. **Speak up.** Next time you witness incivility, disrespect, or injustice in the workplace, open your mouth and speak. You have a voice, and you do not have the right to remain silent.
2. **Make a big ask.** Many people have an unconscious bias because they are afraid to discover a different narrative for people to which they've only known one. Confront your fear of the unknown and educate yourself about people who are different than you.
3. **Confront a fear.** Whether it's a fear of the dark, heights, or human interaction, find opportunities to face up to your fear and conquer it.
4. **Say no.** When someone tries to pile yet another item onto your plate, muster up the courage to say no without jumping through hoops to "excuse" yourself.
5. **Challenge the status quo**. If you see an ingrained habit that needs to change—whether in an individual or the organization itself—get in there and change it. It takes courage to swim against the stream.
6. **Confront someone.** If you have been wronged, approach the wrongdoer. Don't go looking for a fight, but speak clearly and directly about the wrong that has been done.
7. **Share a struggle.** Weak people keep their struggles to themselves. Strong people get honest about their

weaknesses and invite others to speak into them. The paradoxical effect of this is that we will help others find their own strength through our weaknesses.

8. **Stand up for others.** Whether it's the beleaguered barista at your neighborhood Starbucks or the mailroom clerk who just got his head ripped off, step in and speak on behalf of others when they've been mistreated.

9. **Accept uncertainty.** You can't always know how a decision will turn out. Take a leap of faith, trusting you've done your due diligence and have made the right decision.

10. **Lend your privilege.** Understand that not everyone begins on an equal playing field in the workplace and that you may have had some unearned advantages. Once you recognize your privilege, lend your privilege to others so that they too may have the opportunity to thrive.

Conclusion

Throughout this book, we've encountered many people of courage. When we read about people such as these, we tend to think that they've got something we don't. What do I have in common with James Stockdale, an American hero who braved years in a Vietnamese prisoner of war camp? How do I stack up against Maria Montessori, an Italian educator who had the nerve to call out her entire country on their lack of civility? Would I ever have the nerve to buck my chain of command like Harold Cottam? Could I ignore my boss's and coworkers' wishes like that cardiac nurse who saved my life so many years ago?

In the face of these questions, we have to remind our-selves of what I said earlier. Courage is not an innate gift; it's a virtue. So, if you want to become the kind of person who embodies courage in every circumstance, it's time you start developing the habit. Take the list of practices from this chapter and get to work. Somewhere down the line, you'll face a situation that demands more courage than you ever thought you could summon. By taking the small steps I've listed between here and there, you'll prepare yourself to take the challenge head-on without even batting an eyelash.

Chapter 16

Creating a Culture of Courage

In the mid-1980s, Montana was declared a "white home-land" for various white supremacist groups.[1] As a result, Jews, African-Americans, Muslims, and pretty much any other minority you can think of were subjected to non-stop harassment and physical violence. In 1993, the crisis came to a head when a cinder block was thrown through the window of a five-year-old Jewish boy named Isaac Schnitzer. In observance of Hanukkah, the Schnitzer family had stenciled a Menorah onto young Isaac's window, inad-vertently making it a target for anti-Semitism. Thankfully, Isaac wasn't hurt.

When Margaret McDonald, executive director of the *Montana Association of Churches*, read about the incident in the paper, she quickly called her minister, Rev. Keith Torney. McDonald suggested they have their Sunday school students cut out paper menorahs to hang on their windows at home as a sign of solidarity. Torney didn't just agree; he asked other churches to do the same. Within a few days, paper menorahs were up all over town.

On December 8, the *Billings Gazette* joined with the churches in their anti-hate campaign by printing a full-page image of a menorah along with the following:

> On December 2, 1993, someone twisted by hate threw a brick through the window of the home of one of our neighbors: a Jewish family who chose to celebrate the holiday season by displaying a symbol of faith—a menorah—for all to see. Today, members of religious faiths throughout Billings are joining together to ask residents to display the menorah as a symbol of something else: our determination to live together in harmony, and our dedication to the principle of religious liberty embodied in the First Amendment to the Constitution of the United States of America. We urge all citizens to share in this message by displaying this menorah on a door or a window from now until Christmas. Let all the world know that the national hatred of a few cannot destroy what all of us in Billings, and in America, have worked together so long to build.

By the end of that week, there were nearly 10,000 paper menorahs hung up in windows across Billings. As expected, many of those windows were broken. Signs were shot out. Houses and cars were vandalized. Neighbors were harassed. Let's just say the people of Billings were presented with plenty of opportunities to be courageous in the face of intense opposition. But eventually, the violence faded, and the hatemongers moved out of town. The people of Billings had won.

The Courage to Stand Together

It's often said that "the only thing necessary for the triumph of evil is that good men do nothing." In the face of great evil, the men, women, and children of Billings *did something*. As insignificant as these paper menorahs may have seemed, they made all the difference. When Wayne Inman, the police chief in Billings, was asked whether he feared this act of defiant solidarity would lead to more violence, he candidly admitted the greater risk would be *not* to stand against hatred. Those were wise words, and they perfectly describe what happens when we let our Power of One lie dormant as our friends, neighbors, and coworkers suffer injustice.

Indeed, the greatest risk we all face—whether at home, in the office, or in the community—is that we would lose the nerve to stand up for what we know to be right. We all long to live in a community like Billings—full of courageous people who are willing to put themselves in harm's way for the sake of their neighbors. We all desire to work in an office where colleagues are ready to put their reputations on the line to protect one another. We all want to be part of a family that sticks up for its own. But we can't have any of that if we're ruled by fear. We can only have it if we develop the courage to do what's right in the face of so much wrong.

This incredible display of neighbors' collective courage to stand with an oppressed minority and save the town from militant hate is inspiring. As we've touched on throughout this book, we've seen millions similarly rise up in support of the Black Lives Matter movement. Outraged by the injustices they've seen on TV and social media—names such as Tamir Rice, Eric Garner, and George Floyd don't even begin to scratch the surface—these American citizens have said "enough is enough" and are willing to stand shoulder-to-shoulder with their Black neighbors in the pursuit of justice. For those who've been in the shadows for so long, this cultural moment has inspired new hope. Those who've lived in fear are finding new power to fight back against the structures that have held them down. This is what the Power of One looks like at scale, and it's precisely the kind of world-changing impact we can have when we all embrace the power we already possess.

Billings and the recent movement to affirm and protect Black lives are both cases of courage *writ large*. But it's important we recognize that these great movements of courage that bind us together usually begin with individual, interpersonal acts of bravery. On college campuses and in workplaces, a great deal of time and money is spent on bystander intervention training, where we teach people how to look out for one another and step in courageously when they see a classmate or coworker in trouble. This type of intervention doesn't just safeguard individuals at the moment of harm; it creates a culture where people look out for one another. The citizens of Billings, you might say, were bystanders to outrageous bigotry and hate. Their intervention safeguarded lives and saved their city from being overrun by incivility. You could say the same about the millions of Americans who, by way of social media, have become bystanders to racial oppression and are now acting courageously to intervene.

The Cardiomyopathy That Wrenches Us Apart

Before we can diagnose the cultural maladies that keep our homes and organizations from becoming places of genuine courage, we have to take a close look at our own hearts. Throughout this section, we've considered the cost of cowardice and the upside of bravery, but here we need to take a more pointed look at the times when cowardice negatively affects *our* ability to embody courage and strengthen others by way of it. That means asking hard questions about the current state of courage in our lives as we relate to others.

At home . . .

▪ Are you struggling to find the nerve to speak candidly about your needs?

- Do you let your kids walk all over you?
- Have you lost your voice to a dominating partner?

Spouses and partners often suppress their personal concerns in an attempt to keep the peace. Although this is well-intentioned, it ultimately impoverishes the family. The people at home need *you*—not a fearful, shrunken version of you.

At the office . . .

- Do you consistently stuff your ideas for fear of rejection?
- Do you let your superiors or colleagues walk all over you?
- Do you brook secrecy instead of confronting wrongdoing?

You have something to offer your organization. If you didn't, you wouldn't be working there. Above all, what your office culture needs from you is the courage to stand up and be who they hired you to be—not to hide in the shadows.

In your community . . .

- How often do you speak up for the voiceless in your city?
- When you spot trouble in the neighborhood, do you just close the blinds?
- Would you risk a window for the sake of the five-year-old across the street?

The Billings story is challenging because it forces us to ask what *we* would put on the line for the sake of our neighbors. Without courage, communities disintegrate into loose collections of people who happen to live near one another.

Whatever culture you inhabit—whether it's as small as a two-bedroom apartment or as large as a multinational corporation—that institution needs *your* courage for it to truly flourish. For the sake of your family, you need the courage to stand up for and embody what you know to be true, good, and beautiful. For the sake of your coworkers, you need to stand up for yourself and others, giving *them* the courage to stand up for themselves in the process. For the sake of your neighborhood, you need to summon the courage to fight for a community where *everyone* can enjoy all the rights and privileges of citizenship. Courageous culture begins with you.

Rosalind Brewer—the first woman *and* the first Black person to lead a division in Walmart—recognized that the responsibility to impact culture fell to her. As the CEO of Sam's Club (which is owned by Walmart), she used her position of influence to demand that the warehouse store's suppliers begin valuing diversity. Although Walmart and its subsidiaries had already committed themselves to diversity, Brewer's public crusade for diversity in the workplace took a great deal of courage. Both she and the company were subjected to public criticism, boycotts, and charges of reverse racism and anti-white bias. At the end of the day, though, Brewer advanced the cause of the marginalized and helped to create an even more diverse and welcoming culture within Walmart.

The Four Essential Building Blocks of a Courageous Culture

Courageous cultures begin with courageous people, but that doesn't mean they end there. The cultural whole is *more* than the sum of its parts. To develop a courageous culture, you need to do more than simply assemble a handful of brave people in the same place. A culture marked by courage demands intentionality at the organizational level. It takes structures and initiatives that weave courage into the everyday internal workings of the culture. In sum, it takes positive effort on the part of leadership—an embodied commitment that says, "We're committed to building a courageous culture." The following four building blocks are meant to serve as the foundation for just such a project:

1. **Brave Leadership**—In Chapter 14 we considered what happens when fear operates as either a leader's servant or his lord. In a courageous culture, however, leaders must hold themselves to a higher standard. Fear can't be deployed as a cudgel, and it can't be allowed to dictate decisions. Rather, leaders will challenge their own perceptions and lead with a brave regard for others as they seek to cultivate a courageous culture.

2. **Lived Values**—It's one thing to say you value courage; it's another to put that value into motion. To distribute courage throughout the organization, develop a set of practices that embody it in everyday practice. We caught a glimpse of this in Pixar's Braintrust (see Chapter 12). In the Braintrust, employees weren't just invited to give and receive candor; they were ushered into the profoundly unnerving act of having their work critiqued by others. In the process, they were given an opportunity to develop the courage to write a story, present it to a room full of world-class storytellers, defend it when necessary, and receive crucial feedback.

3. **Tough Love (Responsibility and Accountability)**— Similar to #2, a courageous culture needs to be willing to follow its values to the bitter end, even when that means acting against short-term self-interest. Nothing diminishes courage more quickly than inconsistency and special treatment. When leadership stands up, on the other hand, and doesn't hesitate to terminate a high-value employee or to cut ties with a morally suspect partner, they signal to everyone in the organization that there is more to the company than crass self-protection. Regular displays of courage like this give heart to the organization

4. **Rugged Solidarity**—Here, the people of Billings give us a stunning example. In an organizational setting, no one

stands alone. The courage to stand does not exist without the courage to stand *together*. If you want to create a place marked by courage, your people need to know that both you and their colleagues or neighbors have their back—no matter what.

Although much of what I've shared here was framed with a corporate environment in mind, there's no reason why these principles can't apply to the home or a neighborhood organization. Brave leadership is a universal ideal—something to which we should all aspire as we seek to influence. It's imperative that we live in a way that integrates our most closely held values with our everyday actions—whether those values are a family's devotion to mutual support or a neighborhood non-profit's commitment to beautification. Parents need to give (and receive!) tough love every bit as much as a corporate executive does, lest their kids wander off track. And, without rugged solidarity, no cultural unit can survive the challenges that exist both within and without.

Conclusion

In this chapter, I offered the city of Billings, Montana, as a shining example of what it looks like when a handful of individuals courageously take hold of their Power of One and inspire others to do the same. I then asked a few hard questions to determine how we fail to contribute our own courage to the cultures in which we find ourselves. Finally, I described the four building blocks that need to be "placed" in order for a culture to grow together in courage. In all, I've sought to show that cultural courage involves a sympathetic relationship between the individual employee, neighbor, or family member and the whole organization, community, or family.

Paradoxically, the Power of One only comes into its own when it's used for the sake of others. It may be a power *of* one, but it's also a power *for* many. Influence is an other-centered phenomenon, and it only happens when individuals muster the courage to come out of hiding, shed their fear, and do what they know needs to be done. Without courage, you and I will fall prey to the dehumanizing powers of the dreaded default mode. With courage, however, we will inspire ourselves and others to take heart and stand tall. Whether we face the external opposition of racism and abuse or the internal opposition of fear and insecurity, the courage we share will empower us to move forward together.

Note

1. For more about the following story, see www.religioustoler ance.org/menorah.htm. Also, see the TEDxWhitefish talk from Chuck Tooley, the longest-serving mayor in the history of Billings, Montana, accessed from www.youtube.com/ watch?v=8E0JfD8IsE8.

Chapter 17

Conclusion

I write these final words just a few days into the fall of 2021. We had hoped that this year would gently lead us back into the station, but instead it has shaped up to be yet another deep plunge on the roller-coaster. Through all of their ups and downs (mostly the latter), the past two years have shaken us to our core and significantly changed the way we live, work, and think. And even though so much of this has felt like a curse, we've also received a great blessing in the midst of our trial. We've discovered how much we need one another. We've learned to see and appreciate the nameless, faceless delivery people, store clerks, and utility workers who perform the essential functions that keep us all going. We've witnessed the plight of those fellow citizens who once lived in the shadows and decided that we can no longer remain silent. These are beautiful things, even if they've come about through ugly circumstances.

Now is the time for us to continue to rise and embrace the power we have to effect real, meaningful change in our world. Now is the time for us to summon the courage to speak candidly about the people and processes we see around us—in the hopes of creating the civil society of which we all long to

DOI: 10.4324/9781003266556-17

be a part. I began this book with a story about a woman who used her Power of One to quite literally save my young life. As this book draws to a close, I want to leave you with another story that demonstrates how one man's courage saved and altered the course of American democracy. In his story, we see the three C's of influence exemplified and put to use on the national stage. Through his power, we catch a glimpse of the power we *all* have within.

Man Meets Mob

On January 6, 2021, President Donald J. Trump stood before tens of thousands of supporters in downtown Washington, D.C. They'd gathered because, for two months, their president had fed them a steady diet of junk news and conspiracy theories claiming that the election had been stolen from him—from *them*. Now, at this rally, their only hope to "stop the steal" and save America was to march down to Capitol Hill and urge Congress to refuse to certify the results of the election. What unfolded from there was horrific; a mob of domestic terrorists stormed the Capitol Building, many of whom have since admitted their intent to take members of Congress hostage. These members were forced to suspend the people's business as they fled for their lives. The work of the government came to a grinding halt as a defeated leader sought to overturn the will of the people and assert his own in their place. There's a word for that: *sedition.*

Whether Trump intended to stoke seditious behavior is a matter of legal dispute. The House of Representatives deemed him guilty of sedition when they impeached the president on January 13. The Senate said otherwise when they voted to acquit him one month later. We might argue over legal definitions and mechanisms of accountability for a former president, but what no honest person can deny is the black mark

January 6 left on our democracy. We've all seen with our own eyes the horrors of an angry mob descending upon the Capitol Building. We've all witnessed the utter contradiction of rioters beating capitol police officers with a "Blue Lives Matter" flag. We've all recoiled at the sounds of rioters chanting, "Hang Pence!"

But we also saw great courage that day. As the mob stormed the building, one video shows a Capitol police officer being chased up a flight of stairs. Noticing an unguarded door to the Senate chamber, this officer acted quickly to redirect the mob by baiting them in the opposite direction. Had he not, the rabble would've had direct access to the chamber where the Vice President and Senate were gathered to certify the election of Joe Biden. That's how close the mob—fueled by rage, armed with zipties, and eager to "Hang Pence"—came to venting the fullness of their anger on key representatives of our federal government. I shudder to think what would've happened if they had entered that chamber—how the world would've watched on YouTube as domestic terrorists took a knife to the core of American democracy.

But the only reason January 6 will go down as *a* dark day rather than *the* darkest day in our history is one man's courage. That man's name is Eugene Goodman, a true American hero who was awarded the Congressional Gold Medal for his actions in the Capitol. So many of Goodman's fellow officers stepped aside during the assault, but he stepped up. How ironic that, just a few months prior, Black Lives Matter protestors peacefully arrived at the Capitol, only to be met with heavily armed police officers. And yet, even in the wake of *that* injustice, Goodman (an African-American man) chose to do his duty and put his life on the line for a country that so often subjected him to such incivility.

Imagine if he didn't. Five people died that day. Without Goodman, I'm convinced that number would've been much higher. Even worse, American democracy would've died along with them as the mob ripped apart our democratically elected government on social media for the whole world to see. In this, Goodman reminds me of Crispus Attucks—the first American to die in the American Revolution. A former slave, this Black man (who wasn't even considered a man at that time) stood with a crowd of Patriots in Boston and heaped scorn at the British soldiers. He cried out for freedom alongside the very people who'd denied him *his* freedom, only to be silenced when the soldiers fired upon them in an event we would all read about in the history books—the Boston Massacre.

When I think about these two men and what they represent, I can't help but relate them to the workplace. So many marginalized employees have given their all to organizations that barely recognize their humanity. They've missed dinners with their families. They've sacrificed their time and money to pursue extra certifications and degrees for the sake of their work. Yet, they've endured discrimination, harassment, and bullying. They've been forced to accept lower pay and higher accountability. They've been passed over for positions they deserved and thrown under the bus for the mistakes of others.

Let me ask you a question: Knowing what you now know about Goodman, how would you feel if you learned he'd been marginalized by his superiors or harassed by his peers? You'd be outraged, I'm sure. Now, look around your organization. Who's been put down and left out? Who are the potential Eugene Goodmans in your midst? I promise you, there are probably more than one.

A Model Citizen

In Chapter 1, I defined civility as citizenship. Civility is about more than just being nice; it's about subordinating our individual desires for the sake of the whole—in other words,

laying down our metaphorical lives in order to build a civilization in which we and others can truly flourish. Civil people
demonstrate their Power of One in their genuine desire to
build others up rather than tear them down. They do this
because other human beings are inherently worthy of dignity
and respect. They also do it because they recognize that we're
all in this together—whether that "this" is the home, office,
church, neighborhood, or an entire country.

In the wake of the Capitol riot, we need civility more than
ever. The contrast between a mostly white crowd of domestic
terrorists waltzing into the building vs. a mostly Black crowd
of Black Lives Matter activists encountering a wall of police
officers in riot gear highlights the ongoing racial inequity that
persists in our country. How many of those rioters and terrorists walked away without being held accountable? In contrast,
how many of those protestors knew an innocent Black man
or woman who'd died unjustly at the hands of police? If we're
truly going to be in this together, then we need to see these
inequities for what they are and work together to create a
society in which we can all flourish—black, white, brown, or
otherwise.

What Comes out of Darkness into the Light

In Chapter 2, I described candor as the integrity of a person's
speech, thoughts, and actions. In its linguistic roots, *candor* literally means a shining out of one's inner light. Candid people
display their truth transparently for all to see. They speak with
clarity and integrity. They act in line with their stated beliefs.
They don't hold back in the name of faux civility. Instead, they
speak the truth as they see it, even if that means ruffling a few
feathers. Why? Because darkness and obfuscation are the selfish means by which we keep ourselves and others in metaphorical chains. The truth, however, will set us free.

Social media has become our most potent instrument for disseminating information—true or false. We see positive and negative examples of that in the role social media has played in organizing peaceful protests *and* riotous attacks such as the one we saw on January 6. A cell phone in hand, millions of Americans have been given a power that once only belonged to the elites—the power to publish. We need to pay special attention to those marginalized voices who've finally received a chance to tell their story. We need to hear and share what they have to say as they shine a light on realities that have been so long hidden from our view. By sharing these *true* stories, we will drown out the noise and falsehood that plague our national discourse.

A Heart to Stand with and for Others

In Chapter 3, I presented courage as the strength of heart to act on what you know to be right. Courage, in that sense, doesn't mean the absence of fear. In fact, the most courageous actions often take place in the face of fear. I saved courage for last, because I thought it to be not the least important of the three C's but the *most*. Winston Churchill agrees, once saying that courage is the first of all virtues. Why? Because, without courage, we will never find the strength to pursue civility in the face of rank incivility. Without courage, we will never open our mouths and speak out against injustice. Without courage, we will never realize our power.

Today, a sharp word of criticism against what we perceive to be social injustice might stir up a fleeting battle on social media or on cable news. It's difficult to imagine the kind of courage it must've taken Eugene Goodman for him to take those domestic terrorists on a wild goose chase, diverting attention away from Congress. He essentially put his own life at risk. He didn't hesitate because he *knew* it needed to be done. He reached down deep, summoned all the courage he could muster, and used his instincts to save American democracy from the tyranny of the mob.

One Final "C"

As I bring this book to a close, I would be remiss if I didn't mention one final "C"—conscious. In the last analysis, this entire book has been a call to consciousness—the state of being awake. Awake to what? The deep power you never thought you had.

The Power of One is all about being conscious. It's the power of knowing who you are, where you are, and what you have to offer. It's about knowing your everyday words and actions have the ability to create extraordinary change in the world, regardless of whether you've got the positional power that comes with titles, possessions, and pedigree. That kind of power may affect temporary change, but it will ultimately fail to create the kind of influence we've been after in this book. Worse, defaulting to that kind of power gives us an excuse for inaction. When we look to *those* people to fix the world, we justify our passivity. We slink into the default mode, letting incivility unfold all around us. We surrender the Power of One and ignore the people in our lives who so desperately need us to step up.

Eugene Goodman stands alongside the many heroes we've met throughout this book as a paradigm example of the Power of One. Civil, candid, courageous—he wielded the power available to him to save lives and defend democracy against the tyranny of the mob. As exceptional as he is, though, Goodman is neither a fairytale character nor a superhero. No, he's an ordinary person like you and me. Just like the essential workers I mentioned at the beginning of the book, he was invisible before that fateful day. The power he held within is the same power that lies in you. The question is: what are you going to do with it? How are you going to leverage *your* Power of One?

The Power of One is what we leverage when we take a step outside ourselves into a place of awareness, compassion, and generosity. It is the power of words to inspire action and dispel the silence that brings shame. It is the power of our convictions to open doors previously shut by the power of bias. It is the power of our voices to speak up for the voiceless and marginalized. When it comes to the inequality and injustice we witness every day, we do not have the right to remain silent.

The Power of One is not a privilege to be bestowed upon you by someone else. It is a *right*—the innate power you carry with you every moment of every day. It is the great equalizer, for it does not depend upon your job title, bank account balance, or mailing address. If there is breath in your lungs, then you have this power to change the world—to change *your* world—for the better.

Have you forgotten what it means to live and move with *power*? You have something to offer this world—something *we all need* now more than ever. But we can't have what you aren't willing to give. If you and I are going to use our Power of One to create a better world, we've got to be intentional. We've got to be conscious. It's only by learning civility, candor, and courage that we will be able to switch off the "default mode" and become people of positive and enduring influence. No longer can we rely on the superficial power or institutional authority of others to create the world we wish we were living in. Whoever and wherever we are, it's up to us to do that—to infuse our ordinary actions with the power to bring about the extraordinary. As we've seen over and over in this book, we can never underestimate the Power of One to change the world. Indeed, it's the only thing that ever has.

Acknowledgements

In 2018, I was honored to be presented with the opportunity to conduct a TEDx talk at Connecticut College. Over the past several years, TEDx has become a tremendous platform for people to share their big ideas and experiences in the workplace and beyond. I knew that I had a story to share that may inspire others to make a difference in this world. I also knew that there was more to the Power of One than I could ever squeeze into an 18-minute talk. As a woman of color climbing the corporate ladder, there have been times when I have been the "first" or "only" person from my demographic sitting at the decision-making table. I have used those opportunities to advocate and be the voice of the unseen, unheard, undervalued, and underrepresented. It has not always been an easy fight. There have been instances when I have prevailed and instances when I have failed. No matter the outcome, I have acknowledged and used my privilege to cultivate better workplaces and communities. I've used my Power of One.

So many people in my life have used their Power of One to make space for my voice to be heard, beginning with my wonderful husband, who saw a gift in me that I had not yet acknowledged and challenged me to become my best me. Without him putting his career to the side to become a full-time parent, homemaker, and business partner, I would not have had the opportunity to write this book. Thank you, Kent, for the countless nights brainstorming in the "war room" and for making me laugh when I wanted to cry. No one will ever understand the sacrifices you've made behind the scenes of it all. I'll never be able to appreciate you enough.

To my children, Shannon and Campbell, who constantly remind me that the work I am doing is important. Although my work may take me away for days at a time and I may not be a "traditional" mom, you have always made it known that you are proud that I am working hard to create a more equitable world for you to live, play, and work in.

To "Tavie," an inspirational woman who inspired the Power of One with her powerful message "One Can Make a Difference": I hope you're proud and smiling down from above.

Thank you, Kristine, of Taylor and Francis for believing in me and my work. I never imagined when I browsed your website to select textbooks for my college students that one day, I would be one of your distinguished authors. Thank you for giving me your tremendous platform to be heard.

Thank you, Kenny, for being an amazing writing consultant. You bring my vision of the written word to light. You are a gift.

Index

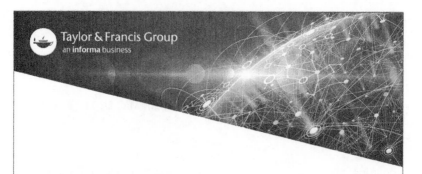